Understanding Abstract Concepts across Modes in Multimodal Discourse

This volume looks at spatialization of abstract concepts in verbo-pictorial aphorisms at work in the cartoons of a single artist. While extensive work has been done in studying spatialization of abstract concepts in grammar and lexicon within cognitive linguistics, this book is the first of its kind to provide a detailed account of such phenomena in multimodal discourse. The volume integrates a range of approaches from cognitive linguistics, including image schema theory, conceptual theory of metaphor, multimodal metaphor theory, the dynamic approach to metaphor, and a multimodal approach to metonymy, and applies this multi-faceted framework to a selection of cartoons from the work of Polish artist Janusz Kapusta. Taken together, these cartoons form the basis of two comprehensive case studies which explore the abstract concepts of "emotions" and "life", highlighting the ways in which cartoons can illustrate the important relationship between space, situated cognition, and language and, in turn, a clear and systematic framework for establishing cohesive ties between the verbal and pictorial modes in multimodal cognitive linguistic research. The volume sheds new light on visual thinking and multimodal rendition of creative abstract thought.

Elżbieta Górska is Professor in the Institute of English Studies at the University of Warsaw, Poland. She has published the monograph, *On Parts and Wholes. A Cognitive Study of English Schematic Part Terms*, and articles on cognitive lexical semantics, word formation, verbo-musical metaphors, text-image relations, and multimodal discourse.

Understanding Abstract Concepts across Modes in Multimodal Discourse
A Cognitive Linguistic Approach

Elżbieta Górska

Routledge
Taylor & Francis Group

LONDON AND NEW YORK

First published 2020 by Routledge

2 Park Square, Milton Park, Abingdon, Oxon, OX14 4RN
605 Third Avenue, New York, NY 10017

Routledge is an imprint of the Taylor & Francis Group, an informa business

First issued in paperback 2020

Copyright © 2020 Taylor & Francis

The right of Elżbieta Górska to be identified as author of this work has been asserted by her in accordance with sections 77 and 78 of the Copyright, Designs and Patents Act 1988.

All rights reserved. No part of this book may be reprinted or reproduced or utilised in any form or by any electronic, mechanical, or other means, now known or hereafter invented, including photocopying and recording, or in any information storage or retrieval system, without permission in writing from the publishers.

Notice:
Product or corporate names may be trademarks or registered trademarks, and are used only for identification and explanation without intent to infringe.

Library of Congress Cataloging-in-Publication Data
A catalog record for this book has been requested

ISBN: 978-0-367-24482-8 (hbk)
ISBN: 978-0-367-78774-5 (pbk)

Typeset in Times New Roman
by Apex CoVantage, LLC

Contents

Typographical Conventions — vii
List of Examples, Figures, and Tables — viii
Acknowledgements — xi
Preface — xii

1 Introduction — 1
  1.1 Developments in Image Schema Theory 1
    1.1.1 The Notion of Image Schemas 1
    1.1.2 Socio-Cultural Situatedness of Image Schemas 5
  1.2 Understanding of Abstract Concepts in a Multimodal Perspective 7
  1.3 The Data and the Framework 9
  1.4 The Verbal and Pictorial Cueing of Image Schemas in Cartoons—Preliminaries 12

2 A Multimodal Case Study of EMOTION Concepts — 22
  2.1 Introduction 22
  2.2 Data Analysis 25
  2.3 Conclusions 44

3 A Multimodal Case Study of LIFE — 48
  3.1 The PATH Schema and the JOURNEY OF LIFE 48
  3.2 LIFE AS A GAME and A SHOW 58
  3.3 LIFE and the Domains of PAINTING and SOUND 64
  3.4 Conclusions 67

| 4 | **Conclusion** | 73 |

References 81
Index 92

Typographical Conventions

I will use small capitals (e.g., FORCE, UP, LIGHT, EMOTION, HAPPINESS, LIFE) to indicate conceptual entities ([image-schematic] concepts, domains and their elements, models, frames) including metaphors and metonymies as conceptual mechanisms (e.g., EMOTIONS ARE FORCES, HAPPINESS IS UP, LIFE IS LIGHT); these will be distinguished from linguistic expressions, which are indicated by italics (e.g., *force, up, light, emotion, happiness, life*), and from objects in the real world, which are indicated by normal lower-case letters (e.g., force, being up, light, emotion, happiness, life).

Examples, Figures, and Tables

Examples (all examples reprinted with the author's permission)

1.1 *"Można zrobić wiele błędów, ale nie warto się pomylić"*—
'You can make many errors, but it's not worth being mistaken' 13

1.2 "Niespełnione marzenia dręczą nie mniej niż koszmary przeszłości"—'Unfulfilled dreams torment you no less than the nightmares of the past' 14

1.3 *"Człowiek jak butelka—ma znaczenie. Dopóki ma coś w sobie"*—'A person like a bottle—has significance. As long as there is something inside (lit. Until he/it has something inside)' 16

2.1 *"Zbliżenie ma swój limit. Oddalenie nie zna granic"*—'Emotional/interpersonal closeness has its limits. Emotional/interpersonal distance knows no boundaries (lit. Getting close has its limit. Going away knows no boundaries)' 26

2.2 *"Nic nie łączy bardziej ludzi niż uczucie i nic też ich bardziej nie rozdziela"*—'Nothing links people more and nothing pushes them apart more than an emotion' 27

2.3 *"Samotność to stabilny stan człowieka, często nienaturalnie zachwiany, przyjaźniami, spotkaniami lub małżeństwem"*—'Loneliness is the stable state of a human being, sometimes unnaturally shaken by friendships, meetings, or marriage' 30

2.4 *"Zakochanie—odwrotnie niż grawitacja. Przyciąga im bardziej oddalonych tym silniej"*—'Falling in love—conversely to gravitation. It attracts more, the more distant they are' 33

2.5 *"Miłość to grawitacja wszechświatów o twarzach ludzi"*—'Love is gravitation of universes with a human face' 34

Examples, Figures, and Tables ix

2.6 "*Miłość jest ogniem, który gasi pragnienie*"—'Love is fire which satisfies one's desire (lit. extinguishes one's thirst)' 35
2.7 "*W miłości świat się zawęża do drugiej osoby, w bólu do siebie*"—'In love the world narrows to another person, in pain to oneself' 36
2.8 "*Szczęście to linia rozpięta nad przepaścią, nieszczęście to przepaść rozpostarta pod liną*"—'Happiness is a line stretched across a precipice, unhappiness is a precipice extending below a rope' 38
2.9 (a) and (b) "*Prawdziwe zmartwienia podróżują razem z nami*"—'Real worries travel with us' 40
2.10 "*Nadzieja poszerza, rozpacz zawęża*"—'Hope opens (sth) up, despair closes (sth) down (lit. hope makes (it) wider, despair makes (it) narrower)' 43
3.1 "*Świat dokądś zmierza, co wcale nie oznacza, że idziemy w tym samym kierunk*"—'The world is heading somewhere, which does not mean that we are going in the same direction' 49
3.2 "*Chociaż mamy nieskończoną ilość dróg do wyboru i tak pójdziemy tylko jedną*"—'Even though we have an infinite number of paths to choose from, we will follow only one' 51
3.3 "*W podróży życia wszystkie bilety są w jedną stronę*"—'In the journey of life, all tickets are one-way' 53
3.4 "*W podróży przez życie to my sami jesteśmy zmieniającym się krajobrazem*"—'In the journey through life, it's us who are the changing landscape' 54
3.5 "*W życiu punkty przestankowe mogą być dłuższe niż podróż*"—'In life stopovers may be longer than the journey' 54
3.6 "*Przemijamy przez całe życie, ale pod koniec jakby bardziej*"—'We are passing throughout the whole life but, when close to the end, as if a bit more' 56
3.7 "*Życie jak fontanna—wynurza się z ciemności i do niej powraca, świadome światła*"—'Life like a fountain—emerges from the darkness and comes back to it, having become aware of light' 57
3.8 "*Życie nie jest olimpiadą. Przyznaje o wiele więcej nagród niż trzy medale*"—'Life is not an Olympic competition. It gives many more awards than three medals' 59
3.9 "*Życie jest grą, w której zwycięzca zawsze przegrywa*"—'Life is a game in which the winner always loses' 60
3.10 "*W teatrze życia wszyscy grają główną rolę*"—'In the theatre of life everybody plays the main part' 61
3.11 "*Film zwany życiem potrzebuje i światła i ciemności*"—'The film called life needs both light and darkness' 62

3.12 *"Życie jest jak płótno malarskie. Jeden namaluje na nim arcydzieło, drugi tandetny obraz"*—'Life is like a canvas. One will paint a masterpiece on it, another—a shoddy/cheap picture' 65

3.13 *"Dostajemy ileś czasu na zaistnienie jak dźwięk"*—'Like sound we get a certain amount of time to exist' 66

Figures

1.1 The COMPULSION Schema 3
1.2 The REMOVAL OF RESTRAINT Schema 3
1.3 The Cover of *Plus Minus. Podręcznik do Myślenia* by Janusz Kapusta (2014). Reprinted with explicit permission from the author. 10

Tables

1.1 A Partial List of Image Schemas 4
1.2 The Dynamic Category of Metaphors 11

Acknowledgements

My expression of gratitude goes, first of all, to Janusz Kapusta, the author of the art that I venture to analyse in this book, for his kind permission to use his works in this study. Needless to say, without the inspiration of his cartoon's verbo-pictorial aphorisms, this book would have never come into existence.

I'm also grateful to Elysse Preposi, editor in the Routledge Research programme, for her support and encouragement throughout this project, and to two anonymous reviewers whose expertise and critical comments helped me in improving this manuscript in its earlier form.

I would also like to express my thanks to Emma Harris for stylistic refinements and revisions of the text, and to Basia Kuligowska and Przemek Nieciecki for their help in editing the artworks that constitute my data. All the remaining flaws and drawbacks are entirely mine.

Preface

With the multimodal turn gaining its momentum in cognitive linguistic research, recent years have witnessed growing interest in how figures of thought known as conceptual metaphor (Lakoff and Johnson 1980, 1999; Kövecses 2015a) and conceptual metonymy (Langacker 1993; Kövecses and Radden 1998; Littlemore 2015) are employed in semiotic modes other than language alone. This turn of research is at the same time focusing on the multimodal character of communication, in which different semiotic modes—verbal, gestural, visual, and also sound or music, etc.—combine in multiple ways to express a single communicative act.

In this book my focus is on how the verbal and the pictorial modes combine in understanding abstract concepts that underlie our knowledge about two quintessential aspects of human experience—emotions and life. Throughout the whole book, it becomes evident that what—since Rudolph Arnheim (1969)—is known as "visual thinking" is at its core image-schematic and metonymic in nature.

My data are works of art by a single author—Janusz Kapusta—a master of visual thinking, who does not shy away from expressing in the visual form of one drawing abstract concepts such as hope and despair or the relationship between a single stage in a person's life and the person's course of life as a whole. His ingeniously simple style shows that a few lines of a drawing combined with a verbal aphorism may turn into an intriguing conceptual riddle whose solution may provide a novel understanding of metaphorical concepts "we live by".

Aside from cartoons analysed in this book as verbo-pictorial aphorisms, which originally appeared in the Polish weekly *Plus Minus*, Janusz Kapusta regularly contributes his drawings to numerous journals, including the *New York Times*, the *Wall Street Journal*, the *Washington Post*, the *Boston Globe*, *Graphis*, *Print*, and *Business Week*. However, his accomplishments in visual forms are many. An architect by profession, he is also a book illustrator, graphic designer, poster artist, theatre-stage designer, and painter. His works of art are included in the collections of, for example, the Museum of Modern Art in New York, Museum of Modern Art in San Francisco, IBM Collection, the Museum of Art in Lodz, Galerie Roi Doré in Paris, and the Getullio Alvani Collection, Italy. But perhaps the most outstanding achievement of his visual thinking was his discovery of what he refers to as an "overlooked shape"—an eleven-sided geometrical figure called K-dron. Having marvelous spatial qualities, K-drons found their practical application in architecture and gave inspiration to different forms of visual art, such as sculpture and painting.

1 Introduction

Against the background of research into image schemas (Johnson 1987), this chapter introduces the theoretical frame for the case studies in Chapters 2 and 3. The data sample of cartoons by Janusz Kapusta, a Polish artist, is described, and a preliminary is given to how the interaction of the verbal and pictorial modalities will be studied in the following chapters. The discussion focuses on the role of image-schematic metaphors in spatial construals of abstract concepts in Janusz Kapusta's cartoons, which are treated here as a more specific genre of verbo-pictorial aphorisms. The method of analysis is exemplified with three verbo-pictorial aphorisms that provide a novel understanding of the concepts of ERRORS, NIGHTMARES, UNFULFILLED DREAMS, and of SIGNIFICANCE OF A HUMAN BEING. In contrast to the gestural medium, films and music, where the relevant elements of image-schematic source domains of a metaphor are never fully available at once, the verbo-pictorial aphorisms provide access to a conceptual image which can be inspected as a single gestalt. Crucially, it is the static composition of verbo-pictorial aphorisms as a genre that makes them a valuable source of data for investigating the question of how the pictorial and the verbal modality interact in understanding abstract ideas in multimodal discourse.

1.1 Developments in Image Schema Theory

1.1.1 The Notion of Image Schemas

In cognitive linguistics, the notion of "image schemas" was first extensively discussed by Mark Johnson (1987) in his book *The Body in the Mind*.[1] The title of the book directly addresses two inseparable aspects of such schemas: they emerge from preconceptual "bodily" experience, i.e. perceptual interactions and motor programs, and, at the same time, they are "in the mind"— i.e. they are patterns of thought that stay "directly" meaningful throughout our life, providing highly schematic structure to both our experience and to our concepts. To illustrate the emergence of image schemas, let us first consider the NEAR-FAR schema.[2] Its direct bodily motivation derives from the infant's primary experience of physical closeness with people, in which physical proximity is strongly correlated with affection and emotional "warmth". In turn, perception of the world around us—flocks of birds flying, or dogs, in contrast to cats, emitting similar sounds, provides numerous examples of physical closeness and distance (along some dimension) being correlated with, respectively, similarity and difference. It is notable that in Johnson's monograph (2007), the NEAR-FAR schema is not mentioned, yet there a schema appears labelled as "TOWARD-AWAY FROM" (Johnson 2007, 21), which implicitly refers to 'moving closer/moving away from'. It would seem, then, that this label names the dynamic aspect of the NEAR-FAR schema which, as any other image schema, characterizes both states and processes. In other words, irrespective of the label, this preconceptual structure captures not only our knowledge about locations of things in terms of distance, but also about things getting closer or moving apart.

The dynamic aspect of the BALANCE schemas is also highly conspicuous (Johnson 1987, 74–76). Aside from the experiential knowledge about the state of balance, it also grasps the preconceptual knowledge about the body losing balance and falling, or seeking balance and finding balance that every infant acquires as it learns to walk. Clearly, "balancing is an activity we learn with our bodies and not by grasping a set of rules or concepts" (Johnson 1987, 75). Moreover, being in a state of balance gains its direct meaning for us also through the closely related experience of bodily equilibrium, or loss of equilibrium, as when we feel that our hands are too hot or too cold.

In turn, when discussing the emergence of the FORCE schema, Johnson (2007) observes:

> Because of our ongoing bodily encounter with physical forces that push and pull us, we experience the image-schematic structures of [among others] COMPULSION, ATTRACTION, [. . .] BLOCKAGE OF MOVEMENT, [and THE REMOVAL OF RESTRAINT] [. . .].The bodily logic of such force schemas will give rise to specific inferences that we draw, based on the internal structure of the schemas. For instance, objects move at varying speeds, they move along trajectories, there is a rhythmic flow to their movement, they start and stop, etc. Based on these and other characteristics of moving objects, the internal structures of the image schemas for forced movement support and constrain the precise inferences we make about our experience. There are thus quite distinctive patterns and logics to these dimensions of our perception of moving objects, our kinaesthetic sense of our own motion, and our proprioceptive sense of the position and movement of our body parts.
>
> (Johnson 2007, 137)

To exemplify the subtypes of FORCE, let us consider the COMPULSION and the REMOVAL OF RESTRAINT schemas. The COMPULSION schema emerges from our experience of various kinds of external force that cause us to move—be they natural forces such as wind, physical objects, or other people (Johnson 1987, 45). The internal structure of this schema is represented in Figure 1.1, where the solid arrow represents an actual force factor, and the broken arrow a potential force vector or trajectory:

In turn, the REMOVAL OF RESTRAINT schema emerges from our everyday experience of actual barriers being removed (as when the door opens and we can enter a house) or potential barriers simply not being in our way (as when a child learning to walk is not stopped by a parent), and in effect a path is open and a force can be exerted freely. The internal structure of this schema is diagrammed in Figure 1.2, where the solid arrow and broken arrow represent, respectively, an actual and a potential force vector or trajectory, while the vertical rectangle represents the actual or potential barrier:

Likewise, the internal logic of the SOURCE-PATH-GOAL schema (a.k.a. PATH) emerges from our ubiquitous preconceptual experience of locomotion: we start to move at some specific point in space and, as we move, we traverse a series of contiguous locations that lead to our destination, or the endpoint of the path (see Johnson 1987, 113–117). To characterize the logic of this schema, Johnson resorts to the following simple example: "Consider a case in which you are moving along a linear path toward a destination, and at time T1 you are halfway to the destination. If you then travel farther along the path and reach time T2, you will be closer to your destination at T2 than you were

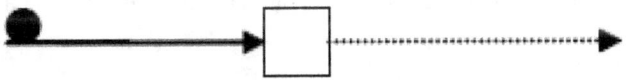

Figure 1.1 The COMPULSION Schema
Source: Johnson (1987, 45); adapted from Evans and Green (2006, 188).

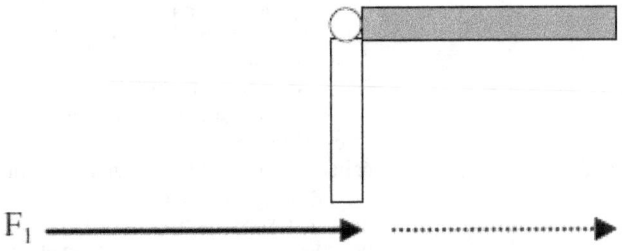

Figure 1.2 The REMOVAL OF RESTRAINT Schema
Source: Johnson (1987, 47); adapted from Evans and Green (2006, 189).

at T1" (2007, 139). However "trivial" it may sound, he goes on to argue, "it is just such spatial and bodily logic that makes it possible for us to make sense of, and to act intelligently within, our ordinary experience" (Johnson 2007, 139). Note, further, that relative to the PATH schema we also derive inferences about motions without any clear goal. And, through our experience of rectilinear motion, we arrive at more specific inferences about the straight-line movement, curved motions, or other deviations from motion along a straight path (Cienki 1998b).

Over the years, the list of image schemas has been expanded. Johnson's original "partial list" names 27 (1987, 126), while the list compiled from the available literature by Evans and Green (2006) includes 40 (see Table 1.1).[3] Note that in Table 1.1 the schemas are arranged in terms of their experiential grounding; the NEAR-FAR and the PATH schemas are included in, respectively, the "spatial" and the "locomotion" group, while BALANCE and FORCE constitute two distinct subgroups.

Experientially, image schemas commonly cluster together, forming gestalt structures (Cienki 1997). For example, the cluster of CENTRE-PERIPHERY, NEAR-FAR, SCALE, and FORCE schemas forms one common experiential gestalt: "In our bodily experience, we are centres of force, sources of movement and action. While on one hand, each of us is subjected to many external forces on a daily basis (literally or metaphorically), the individual is also a starting point of vectors of force, which can be exerted outward from the body, and which typically decrease in intensity the further out they extend (hence their scalar nature)" (Cienki 1997, 8). The grouping of CYCLE, PATH, PROCESS, ITERATION, and FORCE is another common experiential gestalt: "A CYCLE can be understood as a PATH that returns to its point of origin, representing a PROCESS

Table 1.1 A Partial List of Image Schemas

space	front-back, left-right, up-down (verticality), near-far, centre-periphery, contact, straight
containment	container, in-out, surface, full-empty, content
locomotion	source-path-goal, momentum
balance	equilibrium, axis balance, twin-balance, point-balance
force	compulsion, blockage, counterforce, diversion, removal of restraint, enablement, attraction, resistance
unity/multiplicity	collection, part-whole, merging, splitting, link(age), iteration, count-mass
identity	matching, superimposition
existence	bounded space, object, process, cycle, removal

Source: adapted from Evans and Green (2006, 190, Table 6.3)

which can be repeated (ITERATION) and continued by virtue of the FORCE of momentum (Cienki 1997, 8). Such groupings are deeply engrained in our experientially derived knowledge, so that, as Cienki observes, "we are often not consciously aware of encountering them simultaneously" (p. 8). This, of course, makes the task of employing image schemas for analytical and explanatory purposes highly demanding. The difficulty of the task, however, should not prevent us from trying to decompose such experiential wholes with the due attention that this task deserves. If image schemas, as cognitive linguists extensively argue, provide structure and logic to our abstract thought (Johnson 1987, 2007; Lakoff and Johnson 1999), we have to address this task in order to understand the way we think.

1.1.2 Socio-Cultural Situatedness of Image Schemas

It might be instructive to refer, first, to Johnson's (1987) original characterization of image schemas. When introducing this concept, he defined them as "patterns of embodied experience and preconceptual structures of our sensibility (i.e., our mode of perception, or orienting ourselves, and of interacting with other objects, events, or persons)", but, at the same time, he noted that "[t]hese embodied patterns do not remain private or peculiar to the person who experiences them. Our community helps us interpret and codify many of our felt patterns. They become shared cultural modes of experience and help to determine the nature of our meaningful, coherent understanding of our 'world'" (Johnson 1987, 14).

In line with this view, when image schemas were employed in cognitive descriptions of language, the main emphasis was put on their "embodied" and "preconceptual" character, and socio-cultural situatedness entered the discussion in the context of the question of how, within the "range of possible patterns of understanding and reasoning" that are established by image schemas, meaning that is embedded "within culture, language, institutions, and historical traditions" arises (Johnson 1987, 137).[4]

The first work that argued for an extended conception of embodiment of image schemas was, to my knowledge, Sinha and Jensen de López's (2000) experimental study on the acquisition of the CONTAINMENT schema by children from two different languages and cultures: Danish and Zapotec.[5] Relying on a series of experiments that involved canonical containers, they show that Danish and Zapotec children have "slightly but significantly different conceptualizations of 'containment'" (2000, 35–36),[6] and they attribute this difference to the way in which people interact with containers in these cultures. "The Zapotec culture makes use of a smaller variety of artifacts than the Danish culture, and tends to employ them flexibly and multi-functionally. [. . .] baskets are commonly used, in 'inverted' orientation, as 'covers' for tortillas and other food items, and are stacked for storage in inverted orientation" (Sinha and Jensen de López 2000, 35). On their account, then, it is this effect of "nonlinguistic sociocultural difference regarding canonical artifact use" that speaks for extending "embodiment" beyond the "humanly corporeal" and for attributing it also to everyday artifacts. Crucially, such "embodied artifacts" evoke characteristic cultural models of how people interact with them, and in this way, as Sinha and Jensen de López claim, they may themselves shape image-schematic thought. In brief, the extended embodiment thesis "does not see cognitive mappings in terms of a one-way street from individual (embodied domains) to society (abstract and social domains)" (Sinha and Jensen de López 2000, 20), but opens a path going in the opposite direction as well.[7]

This stance was also taken by Michael Kimmel (2005), who, considering developmental and ethnographic data, focused on "how image schemas structurally couple with cultural (or natural) environments and thus take on a situated ontology" (2005, 296). Like Sinha and Jensen de López, he advocates a "balanced view", claiming that "cognitive linguistics must overcome a tendency to unidirectionally theorize how image schemas shape discourse, while neglecting how discourse, ritual, and material culture shape image schemas" (Kimmel 2005, 299).

It is remarkable that, as compared to his original conception (1987), Johnson in his monograph from 2007 himself develops a more flexible approach to image schemas. His definition states: "An image schema is a dynamic, recurring pattern of organism-environment interactions" (2007, 136) and accommodates the "environments" that are not only "physical and biological" but also "social and cultural" (Johnson 2007, 151). He argues further that "[c]ultural artifacts and practices—for example, language, architecture, music, art, ritual acts, and public institutions—preserve aspects of meaning as objective features of the world" (Johnson 2007, 151).

The tight link between corporeal embodiment and culture has gained focal attention in recent research on image-schematic metaphors, i.e. metaphors that evoke an image schema or an image schema complex as their source domain and whose function is to highlight some aspect or aspects of an abstract target concept (Johnson 1987; Lakoff and Johnson 1999). To illustrate this trend, let me refer to a study by Winter and Matlock (2017), where the authors explicitly argue for "a cultural feedback loop" (2017, 108–112).[8] They claim that "from the perspective of a learning child, there is no principled difference between environmental correlations commonly subsumed under the 'embodied origins' of primary metaphors and the cultural correlations" (2017, 109).[9] When discussing such correlations, they also consider cultural reflections of the primary metaphor SOCIAL DISTANCE IS PHYSICAL DISTANCE.[10] They mention here two tendencies in human relationships that are

Introduction 7

known in social science under the rubric of "segregation effects" and "peer effects". These tendencies—for people to move physically close to others they perceive as similar (or feel intimate with) and to adopt certain behaviours from them, and in effect become more like them—give rise to large scale correlations of social distance and intimacy, on the one hand, and physical distance on the other hand (Winter and Matlock 2017, 104).

A different form of cultural representation where this metaphor commonly shows up is film. When concluding their analysis of one example from this genre—a scene about two characters in a stormy emotional relationship (from the film *Before Midnight*), Winter and Matlock say: "both the relative positioning of the characters and the position of (and perspective taken by) the camera adhere to SOCIAL DISTANCE IS PHYSICAL DISTANCE" (2017, 105). And, more generally, in film-making, visual realizations of this primary metaphor, similarly to visual manifestations of numerous other primary metaphors (such as: BAD IS DARK, IMPORTANCE IS SIZE/VOLUME, NORMAL IS STRAIGHT, RELATIONSHIPS ARE ENCLOSURES) are used as *mise-en-scène* techniques "so often that they have become clichés" (Ortiz 2014, 5).

And so being exposed to cultural correlations of this kind on an everyday basis, we grow up in what Winter and Matlock call "a metaphor infused culture" which, through such correlations, constantly "reminds" us of the metaphorical mappings we learned when we were very young (see Winter and Matlock 2017, 109). At the same time, the fact that we live in a metaphor infused culture has, as Winter and Matlock observe, another important consequence: it might be difficult, if not impossible, to tease apart the corporeal and the cultural motivation and design an experiment that would test a strictly "embodied" origin of primary metaphors,[11] i.e. one that would test their image-schematic grounding (in the narrow sense of this term) and nothing else.

1.2 Understanding of Abstract Concepts in a Multimodal Perspective

In cognitive linguistics, understanding of abstract concepts in terms of knowledge derived from our physical experience of space was adopted as the fundamental assumption grounding the spatial foundations of language which, ever since the mid 1980s (Johnson 1987; Langacker 1987; Lakoff 1987; Heine 1997), formed the cornerstone of research on grammar and lexicon. As in lexico-grammatical studies, in conceptual metaphor theory the spatial rooting of abstract thought has been commonly addressed on the basis of linguistic data alone (Lakoff and Johnson 1980, 1999; Kövecses 2000). In this book, taking a multimodal approach to metaphor (Forceville 1996; Müller 2008a; Cienki and Müller 2008b; Forceville and Urios-Aparisi 2009b; Pinar Sanz 2013;

8 Introduction

Górska 2010, 2014a, 2014b, 2017a, 2017b, 2018a), I will focus on spatialization of abstract concepts (such as LONELINESS, LOVE, PAIN, HAPPINESS, WORRIES, HOPE, DESPAIR, and LIFE) in cartoons by means of metaphors having image schemas (see section 1.1) as their source domains. Adopting Forceville and Urios-Aparisi's characterization of multimodal metaphors for the present purpose, we can say that the defining feature of such image-schematic metaphors is that their target concept as well as the image-schematic source domain are "rendered exclusively or predominantly in two different modes/modalities" (2009a, 4).[12] As compared to their purely verbal manifestations, multimodal realizations of image-schematic metaphors have received far less attention in cognitive linguistics than they would deserve. Still the diversity of the relevant research is remarkable. Suffice it to mention here studies on co-speech gesture by Cienki (2005, 2013), Calbris (2008), and Mittelberg (2010); on gestural enactment of Paul Klee's pictures and their descriptions by Mittelberg (2013); on film documentaries Forceville (2006, 2011b); on animation films by Forceville (2013, 2016a, 2017), Forceville and Jeulink (2011), and Forceville and Paling (2018); on music by Zbikowski (2000, 2009), Johnson and Larson (2003), and Górska (2010, 2014a, 2014b, 2018c); on commercial brands and logos by Pérez Hernández (2013, 2014);[13] and on visual rhetoric that is rooted in primary metaphors by Ortiz (2010, 2011, 2014).

Of prime importance for my data analysis will be the ability of image schemas to transfer information between different sensory systems (Johnson 1987). It will be argued that image schemas, since they are skeletal conceptual structures, afford an excellent source domain for metaphors that are realized verbo-pictorially in cartoons. In contrast to the gestural medium, films and music, where the relevant elements of image-schematic source domains of metaphor are never fully available at once, the cartoons provide access to a conceptual image which can be inspected as a single gestalt. Crucially, it is the static composition of cartoons as a genre that makes them a valuable source of data for discussing the question of how the pictorial and the verbal modality interact in the spatialization of abstract ideas. The underlying assumption which forms the backbone of my discussion goes back to Lakoff's invariance hypothesis saying that metaphorical mappings preserve the image schema structure of the source domain, from which it follows that "a great many, if not all, abstract inferences are actually metaphorical versions of spatial inferences that are inherent in the topological structure of image schemas" (Lakoff 1990, 54). It is thus expected that inferencing about the abstract concepts in multimodal discourse will be a multimodal metaphorical version of spatial inferencing inherent in the image-schematic structuring of a particular source domain.

In more general terms, we will see that the discussed cartoons are a valuable source of insights into the relationship between space, situated cognition, and language. In particular, the detailed case studies in Chapters 2 and 3

Introduction 9

will provide supportive evidence for the claim that spatialization of abstract ideas in the visual medium may be independent from how such ideas are expressed verbally. This finding corroborates the results of gesture studies (Cienki and Müller 2008a, 2008b; Müller and Cienki 2009, Mittelberg 2010, 2013; Mittelberg and Waugh 2009, 2014; Mittelberg and Joue 2017), strengthening the view that metaphor and metonymy, as conceptual mechanisms, have their manifestations not only in the verbal mode, but also in other modalities. Since the cartoons also rely on the verbal medium, they offer additional insights into multimodal representations of abstract concepts and the dynamic activation of metaphoricity.

1.3 The Data and the Framework

The cartoons selected for this study, which are treated here as a more specific cartoon-genre of verbo-pictorial aphorisms, are all by a single author—Janusz Kapusta—an architect by profession as well as a cartoonist who has been living in New York since 1981, and since then his cartoons have been regularly published in, for example, the *New York Times*, the *Wall Street Journal*, and the *Washington Post*. For the purpose of this study, however, I have selected a sample of 26 verbo-pictorial aphorisms that were originally published in the Polish weekly *Plus Minus*; the majority of them come from Janusz Kapusta's (2014) book titled *Plus Minus. Podręcznik do Myślenia* ['Plus Minus. A Handbook for Thinking'], which marked the tenth anniversary of his weekly collaborations with this magazine. Out of about 500 verbo-pictorial aphorisms published during this ten-year period, the book includes over 340.

The main focus of two case studies in Chapters 2 and 3 will be on the spatialization of abstract concepts by means of image-schematic source domains, and therefore when considering the drawings I will not go into matters of design or composition which, of course, would be relevant in a comprehensive analysis of aesthetic aspects of individual verbo-pictorial aphorisms. Let us consider, however, some facets of the aphorisms' structure that are directly relevant to a multimodal analysis. The cover of the book from which my data comes may serve as an illustration.[14]

The cartoons always have a protagonist who verbally expresses some aphorism on issues that pertain to human traits and emotions, various aspects of human life and the human condition, society, religion, politics, and the world and universe at large. As the cover of the book (cf. Figure 1.3) makes clear, the shape of the protagonist is reminiscent of a Buddha or a chess pawn, hence the protagonist's aphorisms can be interpreted from two different perspectives: that of an enlightened sage (a Buddha) or of Everyman (a pawn). Functionally, the verbal aphorisms may be regarded as "speech

10 *Introduction*

Figure 1.3 The Cover of *Plus Minus. Podręcznik do Myślenia* by Janusz Kapusta (2014)

Source: Reprinted with explicit permission from the author.

balloons" or "thought bubbles", with the little line segment which goes from the protagonist's head towards the text (cf. on the cover it points to the title *Plus Minus*) playing the role of a semiotic tool for interfacing the verbal and the pictorial.[15] Since in multimodal genres of this kind the verbal and the pictorial elements constitute different facets of a single communicative act, the recipient is invited to interpret them in terms of each other with the aim of constructing a unified conceptualization. The meaning construction amounts here to a problem-solving task—a verbo-pictorial puzzle whose solution itself might be intellectually and aesthetically satisfying.

I will frame my analysis of Janusz Kapusta's verbo-pictorial aphorisms within a dynamic approach to metaphor that has been developed by Müller (2008a, 2017), Müller and Tag (2010), and Kolter et al. (2012). In this theory, metaphoricity, i.e. the process of "seeing" one thing in terms of another, "may materialize in different modalities" (2008a, 32). It is a matter of activation, which is correlated with the number of empirically observable "activation indicators" (Müller 2008a, 198). Such indicators comprise not only verbal means (e.g., verbal elaboration, repetition, specification, semantic opposition), but also expression via co-occurring semiotic modes, such as gestures or pictures. With reference to degrees of activation, the dynamic category of metaphors is characterized in terms of "sleeping" and "waking" metaphors that form two endpoints of the metaphoricity scale. A diagrammatic representation of this category is given in Table 1.2.

Introduction 11

Table 1.2 The Dynamic Category of Metaphors

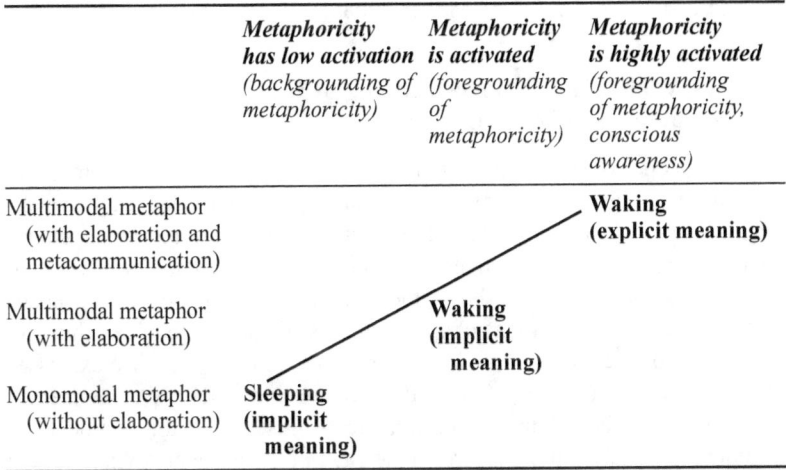

Source: Kolter et al. (2012, 203, Table 1.1[based on Müller {2008a}]).[16]

"[A] sleeping metaphor is a metaphor whose metaphoricity is potentially available to an average speaker/listener, writer/reader [. . .], but there are no empirical indications of activated metaphoricity" (Müller 2008a, 198). A waking metaphor, by contrast, is "surrounded by metaphoricity indicators" and "the more metaphoricity indicators surround such a metaphor, the more it is waking" (2008a, 198). Crucially, any multimodal metaphor qualifies as waking; however, it can be awake to a different degree (see Table 1.2). In particular, a multimodal metaphor whose figurative meaning is only implicit is awake to a lower degree than the one whose metaphorical sense is stated explicitly. Both conventional and novel metaphors may exhibit different degrees of metaphoricity depending on the context of use (see also Müller 2008a, 198). In the case of conventional verbal metaphors, there is one condition for activation of metaphoricity—they have to be transparent, which for Müller means that a parallel literal expression should be available in the lexicon of a given language (2008a, 200).[17] For non-verbal metaphors—whether monomodal or multimodal—the situation is less clear;[18] still, as argued by Górska (2014a, 29), congruent with this approach would be the assumption that a non-verbal expression of the source domain should be evident in a given context through the same kinds of metaphoricity indicators. And, crucially, with respect to the principles of iconic coding and the context of interaction,[19] the hypothesis on gradable metaphoricity predicts that the more cues direct the attention of the interlocutors to the metaphoric quality of an expression, the higher the degree of cognitive activation of metaphoricity in the producer and also potentially in the addressee (see Cienki and Müller 2008a, 495).

1.4 The Verbal and Pictorial Cueing of Image Schemas in Cartoons—Preliminaries[20]

In research on text-image relations, the issue of establishing which elements of the verbal message correspond to the elements of the visual message is one of the main queries. Equally important is the question of how to evaluate the relative contribution of each of the two modes to the multimodal communicative act as a whole. As Bateman (2014) shows, the quickly developing field of text-image studies, while offering a range of approaches, is still at a stage of searching for some well-founded tools of analysis. Similar views have been also expressed by Forceville (2016b, 256–257)[21] and Pérez-Sobrino (2017, 76). The method developed in this book is meant to contribute to this search. In this section, I will introduce my analytical procedure on the basis of three exemplary analyses of Janusz Kapusta's verbo-pictorial aphorisms. Analysis of Example 1.1 will illustrate a variant of the procedure which, as the first step, takes the identification of image schemas and image-schematic metaphors that are expressed verbally, and as the second step, the cueing of image schemas in the drawing; taken together, the two steps aim to establish the degree of activation of image schemas in the two modalities and, in effect, their contribution to a metaphorical and/or metonymic interpretation of the verbo-pictorial aphorism. In turn, the variant of the procedure that will be employed in the analysis of Example 1.2 will begin with the cueing of image schemas in the drawing and then move on to their manifestations in the verbal modality, with the same aim as in the first variant of the procedure—that of establishing the degree of image schemas' activation and their contribution to the figurative interpretation of the verbo-pictorial aphorism. Analysis of Example 1.3 will serve to introduce the third variant of the procedure, wherein the image-schematic structuring of the drawing and of the text are considered simultaneously, and so is their contribution to the meaning of the verbo-pictorial aphorism.

In section 1.3, we have seen that Janusz Kapusta's verbo-pictorial aphorisms always have a protagonist who produces a verbal aphorism that is, as a rule, represented above the protagonist's head and linked to it by a short line segment (see Figure 1.3). Considering, as the first analytical step of Example 1.1, the text that reads "*Można zrobić wiele błędów, ale nie warto się pomylić*"—'You can make many errors, but it's not worth being mistaken' (Kapusta 2014, 208), we may observe that, except for the metaphorical idiom *robić błędy* 'make errors', which is based on the ontological metaphor IDEAS ARE OBJECTS, the interpretation of the verbal aphorism itself does not rest upon the activation of any other image-schematic metaphor. Rather, it is the need to integrate the verbal and the pictorial modality into a single coherent

Example 1.1 "*Można zrobić wiele błędów, ale nie warto się pomylić*"—'You can make many errors, but it's not worth being mistaken'

Source: Kapusta (2014, 208).

message that prompts the construction of multimodal image-schematic metaphors, with the visual modality providing the relevant source domain and the verbal modality—the relevant target concepts.

Apart from the OBJECT schema, four other image schemas are relevant here: STRAIGHT, PATH, FORCE, and LONG-SHORT (the latter is one of the ATTRIBUTE schemas).[22] And in particular, this image schema complex provides motivation for establishing a cohesive tie between the long straight arrow going through the protagonist's head with the idea of 'not being mistaken (possibly in life)'.[23] For the sake of the present discussion, this creative metaphor can be phrased as: NOT BEING MISTAKEN IN LIFE IS SELF-PROPELLED MOTION FORWARD ALONG A SINGLE STRAIGHT PATH. Note that this construal rests on a metonymic interpretation of the pictorially depicted straight line: it is the conceptual metonymy PATH FOR MOTION that would provide mental access to this metaphor's source domain of (SELF-PROPELLED) MOTION (FORWARD ALONG A SINGLE STRAIGHT PATH).[24] Crucially, the construction of this creative metaphor is well-founded in our conventional metaphorical thought. On the one hand, it is motivated by our cultural model in terms of which, as Cienki (1998b, 125) puts it, "normal (default, 'good') action, speech, and thought are characterized metaphorically as motion along a straight path" and, on the other hand, by a metaphor coherent with this model, namely CORRECT IS STRAIGHT (Cienki 1998b, 125). And, by implication, the notion of being wrong or incorrect is conceived of in terms of straying or wandering off a straight path: WRONG IS NOT STRAIGHT (Cienki 1998b, 125). This conventional metaphor quite clearly underlies the construction of another multimodal metaphor which helps in establishing cohesive ties between the text and the drawing: the verbally expressed target concept of MAKING ERRORS can be integrated with the pictorially represented short line vectors that are shaped as bent, curved, twisted, or turned: via the PATH FOR MOTION metonymy, the "distorted" short line vectors may activate the concept of MOTION ALONG A NON-STRAIGHT PATH in terms of which the target concept of MAKING ERRORS is understood. And how can we account for the four short straight line vectors in the centre of the drawing? It seems that the relevant aspects are their shortness and divergent directionality, and as such they can be conceived of as transient departures from a continuous stable motion along a straight and long path of 'not being mistaken'. Note, finally, that in this example the level of image schemas activation is very low—except for the OBJECT schema, which inheres in the conceptions of errors as objects (cf. *robić błędy* 'make errors'), they are cued visually only.

To analyse the next verbo-pictorial aphorism, let us first consider the drawing (Kapusta 2014, 218), in Example 1.2.

With the two vectors functioning as metonymic vehicles for accessing (via PATH FOR MOTION) the concept of GOAL DIRECTED MOTION, the pictorial mode suggests that the protagonist is affected by something coming from behind and something approaching from the front. This interpretation would require an activation of an image schema complex comprising the OBJECT, PATH, MOTION, FRONT-BACK, and FORCE image schemas. One may also assign an image-schematic metaphorical interpretation to the conspicuous black vs. white attribute of each of the two vectors, with BLACK (and DARK) metaphorically associated in our culture with something NEGATIVE and WHITE (and BRIGHT/LIGHT) with something POSITIVE.[25]

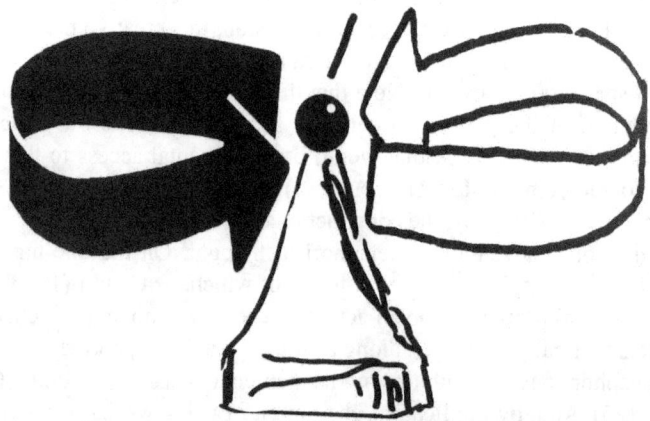

Example 1.2
Source: Kapusta (2014, 218).

When we link this image-schematic structure with the aphorism saying "*Niespełnione marzenia dręczą nie mniej niż koszmary przeszłości*"— 'Unfulfilled dreams torment you no less than the nightmares of the past' (Kapusta 2014, 218), we can now see that the verbal mode introduces the target concepts which are cued in the pictorial modality by the two vectors— THE NIGHTMARES, i.e. the past events are—in all likelihood—approaching the ego from behind and THE YET UNFULFILLED DREAMS are moving towards the ego from the front.[26] What underlies this conception is the deictic MOVING TIME model (Lakoff 1993; Lakoff and Johnson 1999, 139–150) in an extended variant: the future events—our YET UNFULFILLED DREAMS—are moving towards the ego from the front, which is in accord with the conventional MOVING TIME model, but unlike in this model, also the past events—THE NIGHTMARES OF THE PAST—are moving towards the ego from behind. For our purpose, the creative metaphors which make this communicative act coherent can be rendered as: (AS YET) UNFULFILLED DREAMS ARE FORCES MOVING TOWARDS THE EGO FROM THE FRONT and NIGHTMARES (OF THE PAST) ARE FORCES MOVING TOWARDS THE EGO FROM BEHIND. A careful observer may notice also that the fact that the two arrows are of the same size matters—it may be interpreted as a visual analogue of the verbal description of the same intensity level with which NIGHTMARES OF THE PAST and AS YET UNFULFILLED DREAMS affect the protagonist (cf. the expression *nie mniej* 'no less than'). This interpretation would rest on a cross-modal activation of the SCALE schema which, as Johnson (1987, 122) notes, grasps both quantitative and qualitative aspects of our experience of the world "in terms of *more, less*, and *the same*" [emphasis in the original].[27] As for the image schema activation, only OBJECT, FORCE, and the SCALE are cued in the two modes (cf. the objectified *marzenia* 'dreams' and *koszmary* 'nightmares'; the verb *dręczyć* 'torment'; the adverb *nie mniej* 'no less' in the verbal mode and the corresponding arrows of the same size—the force vectors—encircling the protagonist in the drawing), and all the remaining schemas, namely the PATH, MOTION, and LIGHT-DARK are cued pictorially only, hence the degree of overlap is still quite low.

The third variant of the analytical procedure can be readily applied to cases of a high degree of both visualization and verbalization of image schemas, as in Example 1.3. Note, first, that this verbo-pictorial aphorism prompts a construction of a multimodal simile that is cued by means of the adverb *jak* 'like' in the verbal mode and its pictorial analogue in the protagonist's body in the shape of a bottle with some liquid inside.

Clearly, the bottle-like shape of the protagonist's body and the noun *butelka* 'bottle' both express the CONTAINER schema as the source domain of the simile, while the target concept—the notion of the SIGNIFICANCE OF A HUMAN BEING—is only cued in the verbal mode via the expression *mieć znaczenie* 'have significance'. Importantly, it is the pictorial mode that evokes the

Example 1.3 "*Człowiek jak butelka—ma znaczenie. Dopóki ma coś w sobie*"— 'A person like a bottle—has significance. As long as there is something inside (lit. Until he/it has something inside)'

Source: Kapusta (2014, 199).

idea of a high degree of significance by depicting a high level of the liquid inside the protagonist's body (MORE IS UP).[28] Note further that the mapping of the inferential structure of the UP-DOWN schema onto this conception triggers a positive evaluation of the high degree of significance (POSITIVE IS UP). The thus constructed creative metaphor can be formulated as: THE SIGNIFICANCE OF A HUMAN BEING IS THE CONTENT OF THE CONTAINER. Referring to the dynamic approach to metaphor (see Table 1.2), we can conclude that the level of activation of this metaphor is very high for two reasons. First, there is a high degree of cross-modal overlap of the conceptual content, and, second, the presence of the comparative adverb *jak* 'like' draws the attention of the recipient to a metaphorical interpretation of this multimodal communicative act. Let us recall at this point that, in the dynamic approach, the number of such metaphoricity indicators is symptomatic of the level of metaphor activation.

To conclude, corroborating multimodal research on image schemas (see section 1.2), the earlier analyses have shown that image-schematic source domains motivate the understanding of abstract concepts that are expressed verbo-pictorially in Janusz Kapusta's aphorisms. Taking the perspective of the cartoons' addressee, we can thus say that image schemas (see section 1.1) constitute the experientially derived means that we all have at our disposal to

Introduction 17

solve the conceptual riddles posed by Kapusta's verbo-pictorial aphorisms. Since the creative image-schematic metaphors that lie at the core of those aphorisms are deeply rooted in our bodily experience, they may be easy to interpret by the audience at large.[29] Viewed in the context of current debates on metaphor in cognitive linguistics (see, e.g., Kövecses 2008a, 2014, 2015a; Gibbs 2015a, 2015b; Hampe 2017a, 2017b), this section provides supporting evidence for a dynamic view of metaphor (see section 1.3), since the diverse interplay of the two modes in multimodal metaphors—from complementarity (cf. Example 1.1) to almost complete overlap (as in Example 1.3)—points to a dynamic activation of metaphoricity.

Last but not least, with respect to recent developments in text-image studies (Bateman 2014, Bateman, Wildfeuer, and Hiippala 2017; Pérez-Sobrino 2017; Tseronis and Forceville 2017b), two advantages of the method of analysis of multimodal discourse that was presented in this section should be mentioned. On the one hand, by relying on image schemas the proposed method allows for establishing cross-modal cohesive ties which are experientially motivated and embodied. And, crucially, since in this approach the choice of cross-modally cued elements which are analysed as a unit is guided by image schemas and their inferential structure, the proposed analytical procedure stands a good chance of including in its scope aspects of multimodal construction which might be easily omitted in other approaches. On the other hand, the three variants of the method are meant to accommodate different kinds of text-image interactions, with the first variant best suited for their complementarity (Example 1.1), the second for cases where the image-schematic structuring of the pictorial mode is quite straightforward on its own (Example 1.2), and the third one for high degrees of overlap between the two modes (Example 1.3).

Notes

1. The notion was also postulated by Lakoff in his monograph published in the same year, where he resorts to image schemas to provide motivated accounts of diverse syntactic and semantic aspects of language (Lakoff 1987).
2. The schema appears in Johnson's list (1987, 126), yet it is not discussed in any detail. The schema is also known as the PROXIMITY schema (Grady 1997).
3. For an overview of subsequent additions to Johnson's (1987) original list, see Hampe (2005a); for more on image schemas, see Hampe (2005b) and Johnson (2005, 2007). Note also that Mandler and Cánovas (2014), considering early conceptual development, argue that the most basic prelinguistic image schemas are strictly spatial and suggest that the term "image schema" should therefore be restricted to imageable information; a broader socio-cultural perspective on image schemas is discussed in section 1.1.2.

18 *Introduction*

4. It is notable that Lakoff and Johnson (1980) also adopt this style of argumentation. In the context of their discussion of orientational metaphors they observe: "Our physical and cultural experience provides many possible bases for spatialization metaphors. Which ones are chosen, and which ones are major, may vary from culture to culture. It is hard to distinguish the physical from the cultural basis of a metaphor, since the choice of one physical basis from among many possible ones has to do with cultural coherence" (Lakoff and Johnson 1980, 19, emphasis, E.G.).
5. The American Indian language of the Zapotec is spoken in southern Mexico.
6. The artifacts used in experiments were cups (Danish group) and baskets (Zapotec).
7. The terms "extended embodiment", "grounded cognition", "situated cognition", and "experiential cognition" are now commonly used instead of a more narrow term of "embodied cognition" (Johnson 1987; Lakoff and Johnson 1999). As noted by Barsalou, "'embodied cognition' produces the mistaken assumption that all researchers in this [cognitive] community believe that bodily states are necessary for cognition and that these researchers focus exclusively on bodily states in their investigations. Clearly, however, cognition often proceeds independently of the body, and many researchers address other forms of grounding" (2008, 619). The terms "grounded cognition" (Barsalou 2008), "situated cognition" (Robbins and Aydede 2009), and "experiential cognition" (Newman 2017) all refer to multiple ways of anchoring or rooting cognition, which include, aside from embodiment, also socio-cultural situatedness, situated action, and simulations.
8. See also Winter (2014), Winter and Matlock (2017, 110), and the literature cited therein.
9. The theory of primary metaphors was introduced by Grady (1997), and then further developed by Ch. Johnson (1999) and Lakoff and Johnson (1999); see also Grady and Johnson (2002), and Winter and Matlock (2017); for an extensive study of manifestations of primary metaphors in pictorial advertising, see Ortiz (2010), and in visual monomodal metaphor, see Ortiz (2011, 2014).
10. This metaphor is also known as: EMOTIONAL/INTERPERSONAL DISTANCE IS (PHYSICAL) DISTANCE (Kövecses 2000) and INTIMACY IS CLOSENESS (Grady 1997); for more on primary metaphors see, in particular, Grady (1997) and Lakoff and Johnson (1999).
11. See Winter and Matlock (2017, 112) and the literature cited therein.
12. The terms "mode" and "modality", as are common in the literature on the subject, are used here interchangeably; see Forceville and Urios-Aparisi (2009a, 4). It is notable that to "circumvent", as he puts it, "the daunting task" of defining modes, Forceville gives the following provisional list of modes: "spoken language, written language, visuals, music, sound, gestures, smell, taste, and touch" (2016b, 245). For the present purpose, I will use the term "verbal mode" to refer to written language and "pictorial mode" to refer to static depictions of the drawings.
13. See also Forceville and Urios-Aparisi (2009b); Pinar Sanz (2013).
14. I would like to express my deep gratitude to Janusz Kapusta for granting me the right to reprint the book cover and all the cartoons that are used in this monograph.
15. In the literature, the structure of the interface is described in terms of the carrier-tail-root configuration, and the verbally expressed information (typically the carrier) and pictorially expressed information (the root) as well as the tail, which connects root and the carrier, may appear "in a variety of visual forms" (Bateman 2014, 109; see also Forceville, Veale, and Feyaerts 2010; Bateman, Wildfeuer, and Hiippala 2017, 317–320).

Introduction 19

16. The dynamic category of metaphors is from Kolter, Astrid, Silva H. Ladewig, Michela Summa, Cornelia Müller, Sabine C. Koch, and Thomas Fuchs. 2012. "Body memory and the emergence of metaphor in movement and speech. An interdisciplinary case study". In *Body Memory, Metaphor and Movement*, edited by Sabine C. Koch, Thomas Fuchs, Michela Summa, and Cornelia Müller, 201–226 [https://benjamins.com/catalog/aicr.84]. Reprinted with kind permission from John Benjamins Publishing Company, Amsterdam/Philadelphia.
17. By the same token, the so-called "historical" verbal metaphors cannot be activated by an average conceptualizer, since they are "opaque", i.e. their "literal expression is no longer available in the lexicon of a given language" (Müller 2008a, 200; see also Kolter et al. 2012, 203).
18. In her monograph, Müller's (2008a) aim was to give a dynamic classification of verbal metaphors "based on verbal, pictorial, and gestural indicators of metaphoricity" (2008a, 195), and the question of how the proposed dynamic classification applies to non-verbal metaphors was not taken up there. In the revised version (see Kolter et al. 2012, 203), this possibility is built into the model, yet the details are not specified. Note, however, that in her recent work, Müller resorts to "multimodal activation devices" that are used to foreground not only verbal but also gestural metaphors (2017, 301–302).
19. "Iconic coding" refers to a motivated relationship between some aspect of the form of (e.g. linguistic, gestural, pictorial) expression and some aspect of meaning that is coded by the form in question (see also Chapter 4).
20. This section draws on the article "Text-image relations in cartoons. A case study of image-schematic metaphors", which appeared in *Studia Linguistica Universitatis Iagellonicae Cracoviensis* 134/3: 219–228, 2017a. doi: 10.4467/20834624SL.17.015.7089. The relevant parts are reprinted with kind permission from Jagiellonian University Press, Kraków, Poland [www.wuj.pl].
21. Let me briefly explain that I fully agree with Forceville's (2016b) critical appraisal of the method developed by Šorm and Steen (2013) on which the procedure for multimodal metaphor identification known as "VisMet" (www.vismet.org/) is based. Directly pertinent to my research are the following two observations by Forceville: "'visual incongruity' (Šorm and Steen 2013, 26) is not a necessary criterion [for metaphor identification, E.G.], a possibility that is briefly acknowledged by these authors in their discussion section (p. 30). Furthermore, while Šorm and Steen (2013) usefully break down the analyses of visual metaphor processing by viewers into several components (such as target construction, source construction, metaphor recognition, metaphor appreciation), they unfortunately do not distinguish between pictorial/visual and multimodal metaphors" (2016b, 256–257).
22. Note that ATTRIBUTE schemas are not included in Johnson's original (1987) list of image schemas; however, they have been commonly discussed and also applied in research on image-schematic metaphors in user interface design (see, in particular, Hurtienne 2014, 319) and the literature cited therein; cf. also Macaranas, Antle, and Riecke 2012).
23. For multimodal cohesive ties, see Bateman (2014, 167).
24. I adopt here Kövecses and Radden's (1998) conceptual theory of metonymy, which develops Langacker's (1993) account of this process in terms of what is called "reference-point ability". In this framework, metonymic thinking operates within a structured body of knowledge that has the status of an idealized cognitive model (ICM; for the latter see, in particular, Lakoff 1987), and it resides in mental

access of the ICM as a whole or of some element within it via another element of that ICM; yet another option is for the ICM as a whole to provide access to some element within it. The structure which is accessed is called the metonymic target, and the structure that functions as a reference point for establishing the mental contact with the target is the metonymic vehicle. In generic terms, three kinds of conceptual metonymies can be distinguished: PART FOR WHOLE, PART FOR PART, and WHOLE FOR PART. In the course of the discussion throughout this book, numerous specific realizations of these metonymies will be shown to contribute to understanding of abstract concepts in verbo-pictorial discourse. As in Example 1.1, on various occasions it will become evident that metonymic thinking (in terms of e.g., PATH FOR MOTION) opens up a dynamic interpretation of the analysed verbo-pictorial aphorisms and thereby helps in overcoming the static nature of this genre (Górska 2018b).

For more on metonymy in cognitive linguistics, see, in particular, Panther and Radden (1999), Littlemore (2015); for metonymic activation of verbo-gestural metaphors, see Mittelberg and Waugh (2009, 2014).

25. In terms of Grady's (1997, 2005) theory (see also note 9), GOOD IS BRIGHT and HAPPY IS BRIGHT are primary metaphors that are rooted in experiential correlations between bright light and the subjective feeling of safety and warmth, while their negative counterparts—BAD IS DARK and SAD IS DARK are grounded in the primary scene in which the sensory experience of darkness is correlated with the feeling of danger and coldness. Importantly, Grady considers the primary source concepts such as BRIGHTNESS (DARKNESS) as equivalent to image-schematic concepts (Grady 2005, 1605–1606). Following Grady, I will assume that BRIGHT-DARK (a.k.a. LIGHT-DARK) has the status of an image schema.

26. Similarly to the previous example, this construal would rest on the interpretation of the two vectors in terms of the PATH FOR MOTION metonymy, with the DIRECTIONALITY OF THE VECTORS providing access to THE DIRECTION OF MOTION (OF NIGHTMARES AND UNFULFILLED DREAMS).

27. As other schemas, it emerges in our experience of the physical world (see section 1.1), however its basicness also derives from the fact that we commonly experience qualities as varying continuously in their intensity, hence "there is a scalar vector that applies to every aspect of our qualitative experience" [emphasis, E.G.] (Johnson 2007, 137). Moreover, unlike e.g. the PATH or FORCE schemas, SCALE is "value-laden" in that "having more or less of something" is typically evaluated as "good or bad, desirable or undesirable" (Johnson 1987, 123). Not surprisingly, then, SCALE is "one of the most pervasive image-schematic structures in our understanding" which—via metaphorical extensions—allows us "to comprehend virtually every aspect of our experience in terms of SCALARITY" (1987, 123–124). For the role of tactile, and haptic in particular, as well as gustatory experience in the emergence of the SCALE schema and its normative dimension, see Popova (2005).

28. The image-schematic source domain of this metaphor, known as UP-DOWN or VERTICALITY (Johnson 1987; Lakoff 1987), emerges from our bodily experience of gravity: "[b]ecause we exist within a gravitational field at the earth's surface, and due to our ability to stand erect, we give great significance to standing up, rising, and falling down" (Johnson 2005, 20). Not surprisingly, therefore, the UP orientation is commonly associated with positive experiences, while DOWN is associated with negative (see also Górska 2014b). Importantly, these axiological "default"

values of the schema are, as Hampe (2005c) argues, determined with respect to much broader and richer contextualized cognitive models.
29. Research on user interface design has provided ample evidence showing that image schemas and their metaphorical extensions help in designing products that are intuitive in use. Specifically, "[i]t was [. . .] found that task times and error rates are lower when using a version of a product instantiating image-schematic metaphors than when using traditional versions of the same product" (Hurtienne 2014, 320–321, and the literature cited therein).

2 A Multimodal Case Study of EMOTION Concepts

Often evoked to provide evidence for the metaphorical and metonymic nature of abstract thought and its bodily basis in particular, EMOTION concepts have attracted a lot of attention ever since Lakoff and Johnson's (1980) seminal work. Such claims have been commonly based on linguistic analyses alone. This study, by contrast, focuses on a verbo-pictorial expression of two general concepts: EMOTION and FEELING, and a number of more specific concepts: LOVE, PAIN, HAPPINESS, UNHAPPINESS, LONELINESS, WORRIES, DESPAIR, and HOPE in cartoons by Janusz Kapusta, a Polish artist. Relying on the fundamental cognitive assumptions on how we understand abstract concepts, it is argued that Kapusta's multimodal rendering of EMOTION concepts is based on a creative reworking of conventional image-schematic metaphors, such as EMOTIONAL DISTANCE IS PHYSICAL DISTANCE, EMOTIONAL STATES ARE OBJECTS/LOCATIONS, EMOTIONS ARE FORCES, BODY IS THE CONTAINER FOR EMOTIONS. The study thus brings supportive evidence for the claim that image schemas provide structure and logic to our understanding of EMOTION concepts in multimodal discourse. Two other findings further corroborate the assumption on the conceptual nature of metaphor and metonymy and their role in expression of abstract thought: (i) the frequent coding of image schemas in the pictorial medium that is not dependent on how they are expressed verbally, and (ii) the recurring metonymic cueing of such image-schematic domains in the drawings. At the same time, the diverse interplay of the verbal and the pictorial modes in expressing what Müller calls "metaphoricity indicators" (2008a, 198; see also section 1.3) reveals that the dynamic activation of metaphoricity is a common phenomenon in multimodal discourse.

2.1 Introduction

In his 2012 chapter on "[t]he relevance of emotion for language and linguistics", Ad Foolen observes that "[i]n recent literature, the foundational role of emotion is explicitly acknowledged" (2012, 362), and concludes his

A Multimodal Case Study of EMOTION Concepts   23

discussion by saying that the "emotional revolution that took place in psychology 15 years ago has finally reached linguistics" (p. 364). It needs to be emphasized, however, that, providing evidence for some of the fundamental assumptions of cognitive linguistics, EMOTION concepts have attracted a lot of attention ever since Lakoff and Johnson's (1980) seminal work (see e.g., Kövecses 2000, 2008b, 2014; 2015b; Athanasiadou and Tabakowska 1998; Fabiszak and Hebda 2010; Foolen et al. 2012; Zlatev, Blomberg, and Magnusson 2012; Türker 2013). They were used to argue for the metaphorical and metonymic nature of abstract thought and its bodily basis in particular. With the aim to describe their frame-like structure, it was argued that EMOTION concepts are represented as cognitive cultural models in the mind, and that metaphors and metonymies associated with a particular emotion "converge on and constitute the [relevant] model, with different metaphors and metonymies mapping onto different parts of [a given] model" (Kövecses 2008b, 389). In conceptual metaphor theory (CMT), such claims were originally based on linguistic analyses alone, and already in the 1990s they raised doubts on account of their circular argumentation which, as Gibbs and Colston put it, "starts with an analysis of language to infer something about the mind and body which in turn motivates different aspects of linguistic structure and behaviour" (1995, 354). In the case of the EMOTION domain, experimental studies on processing emotional language (see, e.g., Foolen 2012, and the literature cited therein) and on the embodied grounding of metaphorical thought and language (see, e.g., Gibbs, Lenz Costa Lima, and Edson Francozo 2004; Meier and Michael Robinson 2004; Matthews and Matlock 2011; Winkielman, Coulson, and Niedentha 2018 and the literature cited therein) provide one research strategy of avoiding this circularity.

Another way to break this vicious circle is to study how EMOTION concepts are rendered in other modes of expression as well as multimodally. In this case, gesture research has been a highly valuable source of evidence for a variety of conceptual metaphors and metonymies (for an overview see Cienki and Müller 2008a), including those which help in expressing EMOTION concepts. One of the well-documented findings of research on verbo-gestural co-expressiveness which supports the conceptual theory of metaphor and metonymy is that the semantic co-expressiveness in the verbal and the gestural mode need not be simultaneous in real time, i.e., the gestural enactment can also proceed or follow the verbal expression of a metaphor or metonymy (on metaphor see, in particular, Cienki 1998a; Müller 2008b, 2017; Müller and Cienki 2009; and on metonymy, Mittelberg and Waugh 2009, 2014).[1] Likewise, the fact that gestures may enact a conceptual metaphor (e.g., SAD IS DOWN, see Müller 2008a, 80) or a conceptual metonymy (e.g., ACTION FOR OBJECT INVOLVED IN THE ACTION or LOCATION FOR OBJECT, see Mittelberg and Waugh 2009) even when no corresponding verbal metaphor or metonymy is present constitutes supporting evidence showing that conceptual metaphors and metonymies are in fact modality independent.[2]

The modality-independent nature of conceptual metaphors and metonymies also follows from research on verbo-pictorial genres such as print advertisements and comics. For the purpose of the present discussion, it needs to be noted that comic studies have documented two types of visual information which is used to cue a particular emotional state of the character—the facial expression and body postures of a character, on the one hand, and so called "pictorial runes", on the other hand (Forceville 2011a). Moreover, as Forceville observes, in comics "several markers have to be combined to reliably cue a specific emotion rather than another" (2013, 20).

In this study, I will also focus on another static visuo-spatial modality of cartoons. I will take as my data Janusz Kapusta's cartoons that present verbo-pictorial aphorisms on EMOTION concepts as their main theme. Before going into my data analysis, let me draw attention to two aspects of the concept of EMOTION which, as Zlatev, Blomberg, and Magnusson (2012, 433–434) note, characterize our everyday understanding of emotion and are also evident in language. Firstly, as the two main senses of the definition of *emotion* in *dictionary.com* that was quoted in Zlatev, Blomberg, and Magnusson show, our common conception of EMOTION does not distinguish between EMOTION and FEELING: "*emotion*: (i) an affective state of consciousness in which joy, sorrow, fear, hate, or the like, is experienced, as distinguished from cognitive and volitional states of consciousness. (ii) any of the feelings of joy, sorrow, fear, hate, love, etc." (2012, 433). Notably, these two aspects of our emotional experience are differentiated by psychologists, which is evident in Damasio's (2000) characterization of these two terms: "feeling"—"a physiological reaction" vs. "emotion"—"the conscious perception of this reaction" (Damasio 2000, qtd. in Zlatev, Blomberg, and Magnusson 2012, 433).

In turn, as Zlatev, Blomberg, and Magnusson argue, the third sense of the definition of *emotion* quoted in *dictionary.com* indicates that the concept of EMOTION is ambiguous in yet another way, namely it covers both the STATE and the PROCESS senses: "(iii) any strong agitation of the feelings actuated by experiencing love, hate, fear, etc. and usually accompanied by certain physiological changes, as increased heartbeat or respiration, and often overt manifestation, as crying or shaking" (2012, 433). The STATE vs. PROCESS ambiguity of the concept of EMOTION is evident in our everyday experience and in language: "[c]ertain emotions and emotion expressions appear more state-like: *happy; sad, calm.* [. . .] Others like *agitate, calm down, relax* [. . .] are more process-like" (Zlatev, Blomberg, and Magnusson 2012, 434). The authors observe, however, that the process-like nature of our emotional experience is "more focal in consciousness: we typically notice the changes between intermittent states, not the states themselves—analogously to the way we tend to pay attention to motion rather than stasis in the external world" (2012, 434).

A Multimodal Case Study of EMOTION Concepts   25

The ambiguity between the EMOTION and FEELING sense is also evident in the dictionary definitions of the Polish equivalents, as the entries for the loanword *emocja* 'emotion' in (1) and the native term *uczucie* 'feeling' in (2) from the *Wielki Słownik Języka Polskiego* (WSJP) both show:

(1). *emocja*: *silne uczucie, wywołane przez jakieś intensywne przeżycie, objawiające się ożywioną mimiką, gestykulacją, podniesionym głosem, przyspieszonym biciem serca lub wewnętrznym pobudzeniem danej osoby.*—'emotion: a strong feeling caused by some intensive experience which is reflected in an animated facial expression, gestures, raised voice, accelerated heart beat or internal agitation of a person'

(2). *uczucie: stan psychiczny, którego doświadczamy w związku z jakąś sytuacją lub zdarzeniem i w którym wyrażamy nasz stosunek do samego siebie lub otoczenia; doznanie fizyczne: to, czego doznajemy fizycznie.*—'feeling: a psychological state that we experience in connection with some situation or event, by means of which we express our attitude to ourselves or the environment; physical experience: whatever we experience physically' *Wielki Słownik Języka Polskiego*, www.wsjp.pl/

Although the ambiguity of the STATE and PROCESS sense of the concept of EMOTION is not stated explicitly in the dictionary entries, it is clearly implied by the collocations illustrating the usage of *uczucie* 'feeling' given by the WSJP. Consider, for example, the STATE sense in: "*uczucie błogiego spokoju (szczęścia), dumy, litości, miłości, podziwu, radości, rozkoszy*, etc."—'the feeling of blissful calm (happiness), pride, mercy, love, admiration, joy, delight, etc.', and the PROCESS sense in: "*uczucie ogarnia kogoś*"—'a feeling overwhelms somebody'; "*uczucie [miłość] rodzi się; gaśnie, umiera, wygasa*"—'a feeling of [love] is born, is extinguished, dies, expires'. For the purpose of this study I will not go into the two ambiguities any farther as this issue is not directly relevant to my analysis of the cartoons. However, in the course of the discussion these different aspects of our emotional experience and their reflections in language will often become evident.

2.2 Data Analysis

Let us begin with the cartoon in which the target domain of EMOTIONAL RELA-TIONSHIPS is cued in the pictorial mode only, while the two nouns mentioned in the verbal aphorism—*zbliżenie* 'getting close' and *oddalenie* 'going away' are schematic, and without this visual context they could refer to physical distance alone.

The convention of the genre requires, however, that we search for some cohesive ties between the verbal and the pictorial. The dynamic aspect of the NEAR-FAR schema is crucial to account for the message conveyed in this

26 *A Multimodal Case Study of* EMOTION *Concepts*

Example 2.1 "*Zbliżenie ma swój limit. Oddalenie nie zna granic*"—'Emotional/ interpersonal closeness has its limits. Emotional/interpersonal distance knows no boundaries (lit. Getting close has its limit. Going away knows no boundaries)'

Source: Kapusta (2014, 190).

verbo-pictorial aphorism: relying on the image-schematic conception of moving closer/away in space (see section 1.1.1), we can establish two cohesive ties between the verbal and the pictorial mode: the expression *zbliżenie* 'getting close' and the pictorial proximity of the two figures that face each form one meaningful unit, and the noun *oddalenie* 'going away' and the two arrows pointing in opposite directions, another one. In effect, by integrating the two modes into one communicative act we can interpret this cartoon as a verbo-pictorial spatialization of our common understanding of emotional life in terms of our primary experience of being physically close to people with whom we are intimate. This universal human experience provides motivation for a highly conventionalized primary metaphor EMOTIONAL DISTANCE IS PHYSICAL DISTANCE (see section 1.1.3), which, as Kövecses (2000, 92–93) argues, within the EMOTION METAPHOR SYSTEM constitutes a specific realization of the general conceptual metaphor EMOTIONAL RELATIONSHIP IS PHYSICAL DISTANCE BETWEEN TWO ENTITIES.

Turning now to the level of activation of the metaphor EMOTIONAL DISTANCE IS PHYSICAL DISTANCE, observe that, on account of the verbo-pictorial cueing of the NEAR-FAR image schema, the source domain has a high level of activation, however the target domain of EMOTIONAL DISTANCE is not activated explicitly. This kind of activation of metaphoricity is not envisaged in Müller's theory (see section 1.3), yet consistent with this framework would be classification of this metaphor as sleeping since the target domain is implied only.

A Multimodal Case Study of EMOTION Concepts

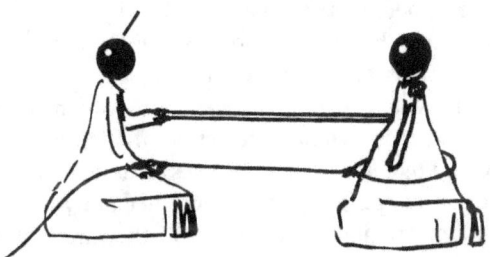

NIC NIE ŁĄCZY LUDZI
BARDZIEJ NIŻ UCZUCIE
I NIC ICH TEŻ BARDZIEJ
NIE ROZDZIELA

Example 2.2 "*Nic nie łączy bardziej ludzi niż uczucie i nic też ich bardziej nie rozdziela*"—'Nothing links people closer and nothing pushes them apart more than an emotion'

Source: Kapusta (2014, 108).

However, the specificity of the genre requires that the addressee interprets the verbally and pictorially conveyed message not at its face value, but as a conceptual riddle that he is invited to solve. As I have already indicated, in the context of what the verbal mode specifies, the pictorially depicted spatial proximity of the two figures that face each other invites the activation of the EMOTION domain as the aphorism's main theme. On this account, then, the specificity of the genre may play a crucial role in increasing the metaphoricity of a message in which there are no observable metaphoricity indicators that would draw attention to the target concept, yet the interplay of the verbal and pictorial cues renders the implicit target concept the focal theme of the message as a whole. In brief, once we assume that this multimodal aphorism draws the concept of EMOTIONAL DISTANCE to the focal attention of the addressee, we should classify the implicit metaphor that provides an image-schematic understanding of this target concept in terms of PHYSICAL DISTANCE as waking.

When compared to this cartoon, the next example can be interpreted as its more specific counterpart: not only do we have explicit reference to emotional relationships (cf. the noun *uczucia* 'emotions/feelings'), but also emotions themselves are portrayed as a causal force that may link people together or push them apart.

Specifically, taking a distant perspective on our emotional life, the protagonist dwells upon the effect that feelings have on people in general, and observes that "*Nic nie łączy bardziej ludzi niż uczucie i nic ich bardziej nie *rozdziela*"—'Nothing links people closer and nothing pushes them apart more than an emotion' (Kapusta 2014, 108). Quite clearly two conventional metaphors—EMOTIONS ARE FORCES and EMOTIONS ARE BONDS (Kövecses 2000)—lie at the core of this multimodal message. Note, first, that it is the source domain of the latter metaphor, i.e. the LINK image schema, that is crucial for establishing cohesive ties between the text and the drawing. In the verbal mode, this schema is evoked by the two verbs—*łączyć* 'link, join' and *rozdzielać* 'push apart, disjoin'. In the pictorial mode, in turn, these two actions are cued metonymically via the INSTRUMENT FOR ACTION metonymy, with the lasso by means of which the protagonist is holding the other person evoking the action of 'linking' and the rod-like object (represented by the two straight lines) that he holds in his left hand evoking the action of 'pushing apart' the other individual. In effect, the cartoon gives a dynamic image of emotions—they are portrayed as causal forces that draw people together or push them apart. Importantly, in the pictorial mode the causal force of emotions is attributed to the protagonist himself—the protagonist is portrayed as acting in a particular way because the emotions "contained" within his body cause him to do so. Note that this aspect of the message reflects, on the one hand, our common understanding of the BODY AS THE CONTAINER FOR EMOTIONS and, on the other hand, our everyday experience of inferring the existence of emotions from the effects they have upon people (in the picture, the causal force of emotions "shows up" in the two metonymically cued behaviours of the protagonist). This experience, let us add, underlies the most common general metonymy in the domain of EMOTIONS, namely EFFECT OF EMOTION FOR THE EMOTION whose specific variants correspond to specific responses—physiological, behavioural, or expressive—that are associated with particular emotions (see Kövecses 2014, 17).[3] Importantly, since this verbo-pictorial aphorism is motivated by the EMOTIONS ARE FORCES metaphor, it may be regarded as a verbo-pictorial expression of the well-established cognitive linguistic idea that EMOTION concepts are "largely force-dynamically constituted" (Kövecses 2014, 17). In more general terms, the EMOTIONS ARE FORCES metaphor has, according to Kövecses, the status of "a single master metaphor for emotion"—a superordinate level metaphor with numerous specific level instantiations, each highlighting a somewhat different aspect of the EMOTION domain (see Kövecses 2008b, 385).[4]

Note now that, similarly to Example 2.1, the message conveyed in this cartoon also relies on the spatialization of the concept of EMOTIONAL DISTANCE in terms of the dynamic aspect of the NEAR-FAR schema. In the presently considered cartoon, this spatial understanding of EMOTIONS is expressed in the pictorial modality as the distance between the two figures; however, the

A Multimodal Case Study of EMOTION Concepts   29

relevant specification of this distance arises via the interplay of the verbal and the pictorial mode. From the "logic" of the force-dynamic interaction that is evoked by the verb *łączyć* 'to link, join' in its spatial sense, on the one hand, and the depicted lasso as an instrument for catching and drawing (typically) an animal closer to us, on the other hand, we may infer that the spatial distance between the two figures diminishes, which entails, in the metaphorical target domain, the individuals getting emotionally closer. This conception is contrasted with the idea of an increasing distance in space (hence, increasing emotional distance) which can be inferred, on the one hand, from the force-dynamic encounter cued by the verb *rozdzielać* 'to push apart, disjoin' and, on the other hand, a rod-like instrument (represented by two straight lines) that the protagonist is using to perform this action.[5]

To recapitulate, the verbo-pictorial aphorism in Example 2.2 is motivated by the well-established conceptual metaphors in terms of which we understand EMOTIONS AS FORCES that draw people closer and establish bonds between them or push them apart and put them at a distance. In effect, two other relevant metaphors come into play: EMOTIONS ARE BONDS and EMOTIONAL DISTANCE IS PHYSICAL DISTANCE. Importantly, the cartoon overcomes the static nature of its genre in that it reveals that forces can only be observed through interaction. This aspect of our understanding of emotional force is conveyed verbo-pictorially: the depicted stage—via the REPRESENTATIVE STAGE OF ACTION FOR ACTION metonymy[6]—provides mental access to the force-dynamic encounter of the two figures, while the verbal modality specifies that the emotions act as the forces in question. We have seen also that, in this example, the pictorial modality relies on metonymic vehicles for cueing the two causal actions of 'linking' and of 'distancing, pushing apart' (cf. the INSTRUMENT FOR ACTION metonymy). In more general terms, such metonymic activation of ACTIONS is a common phenomenon and a characteristic feature of this genre. And, given the affordances of the static visuo-spatial modality of cartoons, the reliance on metonymic reasoning to mentally access abstract processual concepts is by no means surprising. Metonymy provides here a well-motivated "shortcut" to EVENTS and ACTIONS, and thereby to the domain of TIME.

As for the level of activation of metaphors in terms of which emotional experience is understood in this cartoon, two conventional metaphorical patterns—EMOTIONS ARE FORCES and EMOTIONS ARE BONDS—are evoked verbo-pictorially, hence they would qualify as waking. By contrast, there are no explicit metaphoricity indicators of EMOTIONAL DISTANCE IS PHYSICAL DISTANCE and, therefore, this mapping, if evoked, would qualify as a sleeping metaphor that is entailed by the explicitly evoked metaphorical construal of EMOTIONS in this aphorism. Specifically, from the way emotional force affects the individuals, by drawing them together and establishing an emotional bond between them or pushing them apart, we can infer that emotional distance between them would change accordingly. Though fully implicit, this aspect of the construal may further enrich the interpretation of the verbo-pictorial aphorism.

Similarly to the previous two cartoons, in Example 2.3 the protagonist also takes a distant perspective to our emotional life, but this time he focuses on a single emotional state of LONELINESS describing it as: "*stabilny stan człowieka, często nienaturalnie zachwiany, przyjaźniami, spotkaniami lub małżeństwem*"—'Loneliness is the stable state of a human being, sometimes unnaturally shaken by friendships, meetings, or marriage' (Kapusta 2014, 74). In this case, the conceptual riddle seems to involve, first of all, two conventional metaphors in terms of which we conceive of states in general, and emotional states in particular, as objects and as locations: (EMOTIONAL) STATES ARE OBJECTS and (EMOTIONAL) STATES ARE LOCATIONS, i.e., via the metaphor (EMOTIONAL) STATES ARE OBJECTS, the verbal aphorism portrays loneliness as *stabilny stan* 'the stable state' that, similarly to the objects, can be "shaken", while the drawing relies on the location variant of the EVENT STRUCTURE dual (Lakoff 1993; Lakoff and Johnson 1999, 194–200) and depicts this emotional state as a fixed location of the figure in the upright posture on the left.

Example 2.3 "*Samotność to stabilny stan człowieka, często nienaturalnie zachwiany, przyjaźniami, spotkaniami lub małżeństwem*"—'Loneliness is the stable state of a human being, sometimes unnaturally shaken by friendships, meetings, or marriage'

Source: Kapusta (2014, 74).

A Multimodal Case Study of EMOTION Concepts 31

Note that this metaphor is based on our image-schematic knowledge about the experience of bounded spaces, which is known as the CONTAINER (Johnson 1987, 2007; and section 1.1.2) or the BOUNDED SPACE (Lakoff and Turner 1989) image schema. These different labels of the metaphor's source domain are also reflected in this metaphor's different names: STATES ARE LOCATIONS/ CONTAINERS/BOUNDED SPACES.

Note now that the verbal mode evokes an image of a forceful encounter of two abstract entities—'the state of loneliness' on the one hand, and human relationships—'friendships, meetings, and marriage', on the other hand. This indicates that the verbal aphorism not only relies on our conventional understanding of ABSTRACT IDEAS AS OBJECTS, and on the STATES and RELATIONSHIPS ARE OBJECTS metaphor in particular, but also on the metaphor CAUSES ARE FORCES: it specifies that the objectified state of loneliness can be 'unnaturally shaken' (cf. the expression *nienaturalnie zachwiany*) by the force exerted by the relationships in question. The verbal aphorism may thus be interpreted as a creative extension of the force-dynamic EMOTION scenario (for the latter, see Kövecses 2000, 2008b, 2014) which, when conceived in terms of the NATURAL FORCE metaphor, encapsulates, as Kövecses puts it, "perhaps the most deeply seated belief about emotions; namely, that we are passive and helpless in relation to them, just as physical objects are passive and helpless in relation to powerful forces acting on them" (2008b, 184). The verbal aphorism extends this metaphorical model in that it adds a novel mapping, namely, like physical objects whose force tendency is to "keep being the same" (Kövecses 2008b, 385), in the cartoon the Self has a natural force tendency to stay in a stable state of loneliness; however, just like natural forces that may bring about a change in a physical object, relationships such as friendship, a meeting, or marriage may cause the Self to undergo the effect of the encounter and lose his stable state responding to the force in a passive way.

Note now that the pictorial mode provides numerous cohesive ties with the verbally evoked image: the drawing depicts a forceful encounter of the protagonist (on the right) who is falling along a downward steep path leading straight towards the figure on the left. Quite conspicuously, the outstretched arms of the two figures are in a tight grip, forming a small enclosure. We can observe at this point that the visual modality introduces aspects of meaning which are not expressed verbally: relying on the cluster of the LINK and the BOUNDED SPACE image schemas, it depicts human relationships as BONDS and ENCLOSURES at the same time. And, by means of the interplay between metonymy and metaphor, it also provides cues for evoking the idea of the force of gravity; specifically, the metonymy REPRESENTATIVE STAGE OF AN ACTION (OF FALLING DOWN A SLOPE) FOR THE ACTION (OF FALLING) provides metonymic access to the idea of motion (falling down) caused by the force of gravity, and thereby to the CAUSES ARE FORCES metaphor. Moreover, visualizing the force that draws the individuals together as the force of gravity that causes the protagonist to fall down the steep slope, the cartoon opens up an interpretation of human relationships as something which is beyond human control. It is notable that in this cartoon the specific affordances of the pictorial mode show up very clearly: they allow for a simultaneous depiction of aspects of our everyday understanding of human relationships as BONDS and ENCLOSURES (Kövecses 2000). Since in the verbal aphorism these two conceptions are not evoked at all, the pictorial mode greatly enriches the verbal expression and allows for a spectacular condensation of meaning.

When evaluated with reference to the dynamic category of metaphors, the EMOTION metaphors in Example 2.3 whose source domains of BONDS and ENCLOSURES are cued monomodally would qualify as sleeping. Likewise, the metaphors EMOTIONAL STATES ARE OBJECTS and EMOTIONAL STATES ARE LOCATIONS can be classified as sleeping, since each is evoked in one mode only (the verbal and the pictorial mode, respectively). The conception of the forceful encounter, however, is evoked multimodally, hence the understanding of HUMAN RELATIONSHIPS, such as FRIENDSHIP, MEETING, or MARRIAGE as (CAUSAL) FORCES has a high activation level and the metaphor that underlies this construal (i.e. HUMAN RELATIONSHIPS ARE FORCES) would qualify as waking. Note, further, that the two modes give the opposite image of the forceful encounter of the individuals in a relationship: in the pictorial mode it is (metonymically) portrayed in terms of natural force (of gravity), which is in full accord with our conventional understanding of EMOTIONAL/HUMAN RELATIONSHIPS AS NATURAL FORCES.

In the verbal mode, this conventional understanding is questioned—the forceful encounter of individuals is said to bring about unnatural effects in the stable state of loneliness. From this it follows that it is the latter state, rather than emotional/human relations, which is characterized as natural. Arguably, this incongruity between the pictorial and the verbal image of the force-dynamic encounter of individuals gives rise to a humorous or ironic "tinge" of the aphorism's meaning.[7]

As in the previous cartoon, the causal force of emotions lies at the core of the verbo-pictorial aphorisms in Examples 2.4 and 2.5, however in contrast to Example 2.3, in these two aphorisms there is explicit reference to the force of gravity. In Example 2.4, the mechanics of gravitation are contrasted with the way the "mechanics" of FALLING IN LOVE act, which is captured by the protagonist as: "*Zakochanie—odwrotnie niż grawitacja. Przyciąga im bardziej oddalonych tym silniej*"—'Falling in love—conversely to gravitation. It attracts more, the more distant they are' (*Plus Minus*, 30 November 2013). In Example 2.5, on the other hand, the protagonist characterizes the emotion of LOVE itself as 'gravitation of universes with a human face' (Kapusta 2014, 159).

When we now turn to the pictorial rendering of the two aphorisms, we can see that in Example 2.4, the rope that the depicted figures are pulling—via the INSTRUMENT FOR ACTION metonymy—provides metonymic cues for accessing the conception of the forceful physical interaction in terms of which the abstract target concept—FALLING IN LOVE—is portrayed and understood. Note, further, that aside from strengthening the verbally expressed conception of FALLING IN LOVE AS A FORCE-DYNAMIC ENCOUNTER (OF TWO PERSONS), the pictorial mode also motivates the image-schematic understanding of the concept of LOVE itself. In particular, in the context of the verbal aphorism, the rope that the two figures are holding may be interpreted as a double metonymic vehicle for accessing the LINK and the NEAR-FAR schemas as the source domains of, respectively, the LOVE IS BOND and LOVE IS CLOSENESS metaphors (Kövecses 2000). In terms of dynamic metaphoricity (see section 1.3), the level of activation of the latter two metaphors, on account of their monomodal cueing, is lower than that of the verbo-pictorially constructed metaphorical understanding of FALLING IN LOVE AS A FORCE-DYNAMIC ENCOUNTER and, on these grounds, this metaphor qualifies as waking while the other two qualify as sleeping.

In contrast to the previous two drawings, the pictorial mode in Example 2.5 makes explicit reference to the gravitational force by including the gravitational force formula as part of the drawing:[8] the depicted figures are labelled "m_1" and "m_2" and thereby they symbolize the mass of the two attracted objects, while "r" of the force formula symbolizes the distance between them.

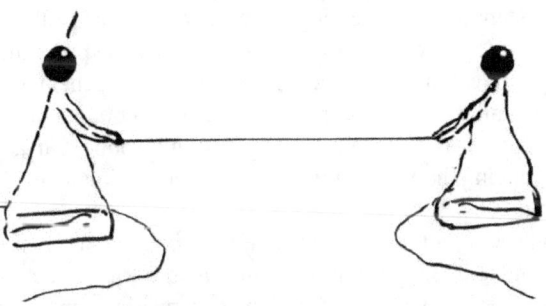

Example 2.4 "*Zakochanie—odwrotnie niż grawitacja. Przyciąga im bardziej oddalonych tym silniej*"—'Falling in love—conversely to gravitation. It attracts more, the more distant they are'

Source: *Plus Minus*, 30 November 2013.

34 A Multimodal Case Study of EMOTION Concepts

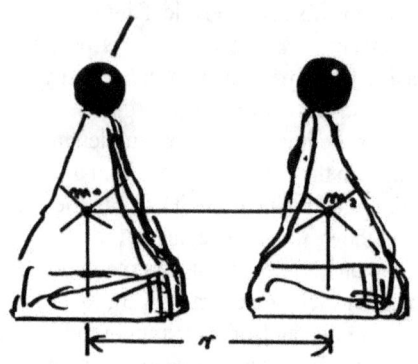

MIŁOŚĆ TO GRAWITACJA WSZECHŚWIATÓW
O TWARZACH LUDZI

Example 2.5 "*Miłość to grawitacja wszechświatów o twarzach ludzi*"—'Love is gravitation of universes with a human face'
Source: Kapusta (2014, 159).

Clearly, then, by depicting the gravitational force formula, the drawing pictorially anchors the verbal metaphor *grawitacja (wszechświatów)* 'gravitation of universes' and, in effect, increases the level of activation of this creative verbo-pictorial elaboration of the conventional metaphor LOVE IS FORCE (Kövecses 2000, 26, 123), whose novelty resides in portraying each person involved in the LOVE relationship as a self-contained universe subject to the dynamics of gravitational force. Putting it differently, on account of the verbo-pictorial construction of the source domain of GRAVITATIONAL FORCE, the metaphor expressed in the verbal aphorism qualifies as waking. Observe now that by depicting the two figures in close proximity, the pictorial mode provides cues for accessing the NEAR-FAR schema as the source domain for yet another understanding of the abstract target concept of LOVE, which is captured as the LOVE IS CLOSENESS metaphor. On account of its monomodal cueing, however, this metaphor's activation level would qualify it as sleeping.

Note, finally, that in this cartoon the verbal mode characterizes LOVE both as an emotion and as a relationship. This "dual nature" of our love experience—the fact that it is perceived as an emotion and a relationship—is, as Kövecses observes, unique among human relationships (see 2008b, 387).

The verbo-pictorial aphorism in Example 2.6 creatively reworks yet another conventional metaphor of LOVE, known as LOVE IS FIRE (Lakoff 1987; Kövecses 2008b and the literature cited therein).

Example 2.6 "*Miłość jest ogniem, który gasi pragnienie*"—'Love is fire which satisfies one's desire (lit. extinguishes one's thirst)'
Source: Kapusta (2014, 96).

The drawing depicts the verbally evoked fire as burning in the fireplace that is created by two spatially close and partially overlapping figures. We can thus observe that the pictorial mode enriches the verbal characterization, since it provides cues for conceiving of LOVE not only as an emotion, but also as a relationship. Specifically, relying on the image-schematic understanding of LOVE as a relationship in terms of the LINK and the NEAR-FAR schemas, the drawing gives grounds for interpreting this cartoon not only in terms of LOVE IS FIRE, but also in terms of the LOVE IS BOND and LOVE IS CLOSENESS metaphors. At the same time, the verbal aphorism elaborates this conception by evoking our conventional understanding of DESIRE in terms of the PHYSIOLOGICAL FORCE of THIRST and portraying LOVE as a means for satisfying the metaphorical 'thirst' (cf. the Polish noun *pragnienie* has the literal and metaphorical sense of, respectively, 'thirst' and 'desire'). In doing so the verbal aphorism relies on a word play that is based on the literal and the metaphorical sense of the verb *gasić* 'extinguish, satisfy', which has a rhetorical effect of reversing our conventional knowledge about fire. And specifically, by the figure-ground reversal the fire is conceived not as what we normally extinguish by means of some liquid-like substance (cf. the literal meaning of the verb *gasić*), but as a means of "extinguishing" one's thirst, i.e. of satisfying one's desire. Running counter to our everyday expectations, the verbal aphorism thus achieves a humorous effect which, let us observe, in the pictorial mode would not be possible.

Unlike in Example 2.6, where the conception of LOVE as a relationship is cued only in the drawing, in Example 2.7 the "double nature" of LOVE—its function as an emotion and a relationship (Kövecses 2008b, 388)—is evoked multimodally.[9] In this cartoon, moreover, the abstract concept of LOVE as a relationship is contrasted with how we conceive of the FEELING OF PAIN. Note, first, that the verbal aphorism, which states that 'in love the world narrows to another person, in pain to oneself', portrays both LOVE and PAIN as states and as forces: the locative preposition *w* 'in', which profiles the inclusion relationship that holds between a thing and a bounded space,[10] cues the already mentioned common understanding of STATES as LOCATIONS, while the causative verb *zawężać (do)* '(to cause to) narrow (down)' gives a force-dynamic construal of these states (cf. two interrelated image-schematic metaphors EMOTIONS ARE FORCES and FEELINGS (PHYSICAL SENSATIONS) ARE FORCES as well as CAUSES ARE FORCES). The drawing, in turn, depicts the effects that the two states bring about: the emotional state of LOVE is depicted as the enclosure of two people within a rectangle, while the physical sensation of PAIN is depicted as the enclosure of a single person (the protagonist) within a circle. The conceptual riddle that underlies the meaning of this aphorism can be resolved in the form of the two verbo-pictorial metaphors: LOVE IS AN ENCLOSURE OF TWO PEOPLE WITHIN A RECTANGLE and PAIN IS AN ENCLOSURE OF AN INDIVIDUAL WITHIN A CIRCLE. This construal is further enriched by the pictorial mode alone: the spatial overlap of the two source domain enclosures—the depicted rectangle and the circle—entails that love and pain may coincide in

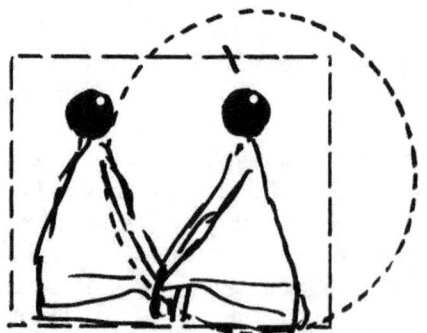

Example 2.7 "*W miłości świat się zawęża do drugiej osoby, w bólu do siebie*"— 'In love the world narrows to another person, in pain to oneself'
Source: Kapusta (2014, 27).

A Multimodal Case Study of EMOTION Concepts 37

our experience, and moreover, when in love, we still experience pain on our own. Note, further, that, due to the affordances of the pictorial mode, we may arrive at a highly enriched interpretation of the two people within the depicted rectangle, which would resort to the well-entrenched image-schematic metaphors: LOVE IS BOND, LOVE IS CLOSENESS, LOVE IS UNITY; these metaphors, let us recall, rely on our very early preconceptual experience grasped by the LINK and NEAR-FAR schemas as well as the schema of PART-WHOLE (Johnson 1987).

And, how, one may wonder, can we interpret the pictorial rendition of our experience of pain in the form of the enclosure within a circle? Relying on the logic of the CYCLE schema (Johnson 1987, 119–120; see also section 1.1.2), we can infer that the recurrence of this state is to be expected. And how can we solve the puzzle of broken lines in which the two geometric shapes are drawn? Why not, one could ask, a solid line? Unlike the latter, it would seem, the broken line evokes the conception of temporariness and the transient nature of our experience of both love and pain.

To recapitulate, the creative conception of LOVE and PAIN which is evoked in the verbo-pictorial aphorism in Example 2.7 rests on a complex interplay of the two modes. As in the previous examples, the affordances of the visual mode allow for a simultaneous cueing of a number of image schemas (cf. the BOUNDED SPACE, CYCLE, LINK, NEAR-FAR, and the PART-WHOLE), which serve to activate conventional EMOTION metaphors and create new ones. Note also that unlike in Example 2.3, where the FORCE schema was pictorially evoked by the interplay of metonymy and metaphor (cf. REPRESENTATIVE STAGE OF AN ACTION [OF FALLING DOWN A SLOPE] FOR THE ACTION [OF FALLING] and the CAUSED MOTION schema), in this cartoon this schema is cued in the verbal mode only.

Finally, relying on the dynamic approach to metaphor we can say that, in this cartoon, our everyday understanding of EMOTIONS and FEELINGS as BOUNDED SPACES has been activated to a very high degree, since the source domain of the two creative metaphors, namely LOVE IS AN ENCLOSURE OF TWO PEOPLE WITHIN A RECTANGLE and PAIN IS AN ENCLOSURE OF AN INDIVIDUAL WITHIN A CIRCLE has been cued in the two modes: pictorially—by the rectangle and the circle, and verbally—by the preposition *w* 'in'. On the other hand, the conventional metaphors of LOVE that have only the pictorial cueing of the source domain (cf. the metaphors LOVE IS BOND, LOVE IS CLOSENESS, LOVE IS UNITY) have a much lower activation level. The same goes for the level of activation of the conceptual metaphors EMOTIONS ARE FORCES and FEELINGS (PHYSICAL SENSATIONS) ARE FORCES which are evoked here in the verbal mode alone.

Example 2.8, in turn, focuses on what seems to be the hub of our emotional life—happiness and unhappiness. Considering, first, the aphorism stating that "*Szczęście to linia rozpięta nad przepaścią, nieszczęście to przepaść rozpostarta pod liną*" 'Happiness is a line stretched across a precipice, unhappiness is a precipice extending below a rope' (Kapusta 2014, 26), we

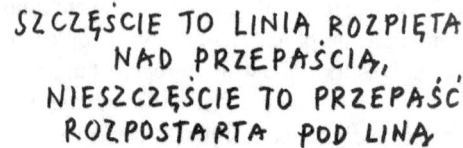

Example 2.8 *"Szczęście to linia rozpięta nad przepaścią, nieszczęście to przepaść rozpostarta pod liną"*—'Happiness is a line stretched across a precipice, unhappiness is a precipice extending below a rope'
Source: Kapusta (2014, 26).

can observe that the verbal mode, relying on the basic logic of the UP-DOWN schema, evokes the conventional understanding of HAPPINESS as UP (cf. the prepositions *nad* 'across/over') and of UNHAPPINESS as DOWN (cf. *pod* 'below/ under' and the noun *przepaść* 'precipice'). At the same time, by resorting to the preconceptual primary experience of verticality, the verbal mode motivates the evaluation of the HAPPINESS and UNHAPPINESS in terms of, respectively, POSITIVE IS UP and NEGATIVE IS DOWN. Note, further, that the text also cues the well-established image-schematic metaphor EMOTIONAL STATES ARE BOUNDED SPACES: the noun *przepaść* 'precipice' profiles a bounded area, while *linia* 'line' and *lina* 'rope', since they are portrayed as extending above it, occupy a limited spatial expanse (cf. the expressions *linia rozpięta nad przepaścią* 'a line stretched across/over the precipice' and *przepaść rozpostarta pod liną* 'precipice extending below a rope').

Observe, now, that it is the highly schematic drawing that relates the two emotional states in a novel way, enriching our conventional image-schematic understanding of these emotions. In the drawing, the relationship between the two emotional states is portrayed by the image of the protagonist as a tightrope walker who is holding in his hands a thin line that represents HAPPINESS, while balancing on a thin rope so as to avoid falling down into the precipice of unhappiness. The verbo-pictorial puzzle can thus be resolved in terms of two creative metaphors: HAPPINESS IS HOLDING A LINE STRETCHED ACROSS A PRECIPICE AND BALANCING ON A ROPE STRETCHED ABOVE IT (THE PRECIPICE). Observe that this interpretation would rely on one verbo-pictorially evoked image-schematic cluster of UP-DOWN and BOUNDED SPACE[11] and a number of schemas that are cued in the pictorial mode only: BALANCE, FORCE, GRASP,[12] SUPPORT, STRAIGHT, PATH, and the metonymically accessed MOTION (via PATH FOR MOTION). And, crucially, it is the image-schematic logic of the verbo-pictorially expressed source domains that provides grounding for drawing a number of inferences about the target concepts of HAPPINESS and UNHAPPINESS and the relationship between them: from the image of the protagonist grasping a thin line we can get a novel understanding of the intangible and illusive nature of happiness. On the other hand, from his balancing on a rope that is stretched above a precipice we can infer that, just like walking on a tightrope, maintaining the state of happiness is very difficult and the effects of losing it are immediate and unavoidable: we cannot but fall into a state of unhappiness.

Observe, finally, that in this example the verbal and pictorial cues overlap in the activation of the source domains in terms of which the creative understanding of the target concepts of HAPPINESS and UNHAPPINESS is constructed in this multimodal discourse. When evaluated in terms of the dynamic category of metaphors, this novel understanding of the target concepts receives focal attention of the addressee, and thereby the two creative metaphors both qualify as waking.

To analyse the next example and see more clearly how the two modes contribute to a novel construal of a number of interrelated EMOTION concepts, let us first consider the drawing only. Beyond doubt, as a highly salient element of travelling, the huge suitcase depicted in the drawing would be a reliable metonymic shortcut for accessing the JOURNEY domain as a whole or some

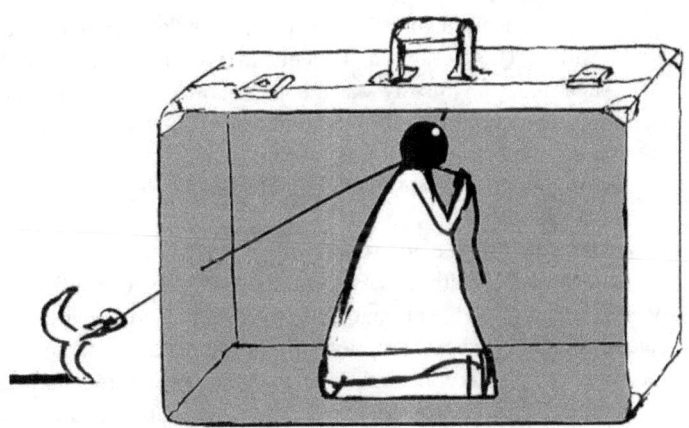

Example 2.9(a)
Source: Kapusta (2014, 23).

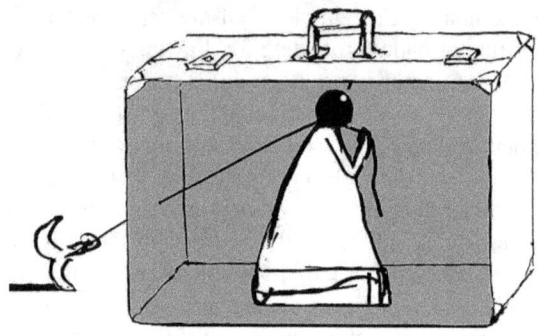

Example 2.9(b) (a) and (b) "*Prawdziwe zmartwienia podróżują razem z nami*"— 'Real worries travel with us'

Source: Kapusta (2014, 23).

elements in it. In turn, the enclosure of the protagonist within the suitcase may prompt a metaphorical construal of a single STATE or a STAGE of some JOURNEY in terms of the pictorially cued conception of CONTAINER. This means, in effect, that the suitcase may function here as a "double" metonymic vehicle in that it may provide mental access, on the one hand, to the JOURNEY domain and, on the other hand, to the source domain of the primary metaphor STATES ARE CONTAINERS.[13]

Observe now that the protagonist's body posture deviates from the canonical upright position. The fact that he is depicted as bending down might be interpreted—again metonymically—as a behavioural symptom of the effort that is necessary to drag or to hold the mooring anchor that he is grasping. The conventional metonymy that would motivate this construal would be, in generic terms, EFFECT FOR CAUSE, and in more specific terms, BEHAVIOURAL SYMPTOM FOR CAUSE.

When we integrate this skeletal structure with the verbal aphorism saying that 'Real worries travel with us' (Kapusta 2014, 23), we can infer that the body posture "enacted" by the protagonist is meant as a symptom of the emotional state of REAL WORRIES that function as a metaphorical causal force here.

In conceptual terms, this construal, aside from the well-entrenched metonymy BEHAVIOURAL SYMPTOM FOR EMOTION, would be motivated also by the conventional metaphors in terms of which we reason about emotional states that are difficult to endure, namely DIFFICULTIES ARE BURDENS (or, EMOTIONAL

DIFFICULTIES ARE BURDENS, cf. Kövecses 2000, 45), as well as SADNESS IS A BURDEN (Barcelona 1986, qtd. in Kövecses 2000, 25) and SAD IS DOWN (Lakoff and Johnson 1980, 15; see also section 2.1),[14] whose source domains are cued pictorially by the image of the protagonist dragging the mooring anchor and bending down. In brief, via the pictorial metonymic activation of the source domains of these three conventional metaphors we can associate the verbally expressed concept of REAL WORRIES with the concepts of EMOTIONAL DIFFICULTIES and SADNESS for which, let us stress, we have no explicit verbal cues here. We may suggest, however, that, as salient elements of the experientially motivated cultural model of WORRIES, the concepts of EMOTIONAL DIFFICULTIES and SADNESS can be easily evoked here without any supporting linguistic context. Note also that, referring to the force-dynamic aspects of the EMOTION scenario, we may also establish here a causal link between different emotions evoked in this frame: sadness may be conceived here as the Self's emotional response to another emotional state—the feeling of real worries (the cause).

Recall now that the image of the suitcase may function as a metonymic shortcut for accessing the JOURNEY domain; when integrated with the verbal aphorism, it may strengthen the activation level of the source domain in terms of which we commonly understand LIFE (Lakoff and Johnson 1999, 60–61; see also section 3.1). Observe now that the size of the suitcase, which has been given focal prominence in the drawing, may be considered as a pictorial cue for conceiving the intensity of the emotion in terms of the BIG-SMALL schema. This aspect of the verbo-pictorial puzzle can be rendered as: THE INTENSITY OF AN EMOTIONAL STATE IS THE SIZE OF THE CONTAINER which, let us add, could be regarded as an entailment of the STATES ARE CONTAINERS metaphor.[15] And no doubt, the fact that the protagonist himself is depicted within the enclosure of the huge suitcase may motivate other aspects of this novel understanding of REAL WORRIES. When mapped onto the target concept, this image entails that the protagonist is fully "contained" in his emotional state. Under this interpretation, the verbo-pictorial aphorism creatively reworks the conventional metaphor BODY IS THE CONTAINER FOR EMOTIONS (see section 1.1.1)—via the figure-ground reversal of the CONTAINER-CONTENT relation, REAL WORRIES are conceived as A CONTAINER for the BODY. In effect, the logic of this verbo-pictorial construal entails that in the journey through life real worries stay with us and we cannot escape from them. This interpretation is further strengthened pictorially by the image of the protagonist who, being hooked up to the mooring anchor, cannot move freely out of the enclosing suitcase. Clearly, it is the pictorial mode which, relying on two metaphors of the EVENT STRUCTURE SYSTEM, namely DIFFICULTIES ARE IMPEDIMENTS TO MOTION and CHANGE OF STATE IS A CHANGE OF LOCATION, cues two other aspects of what might be called the EMOTION frame of REAL WORRIES,[16] namely difficulties we experience in "moving out" of the state of REAL WORRIES and the negative effect they have on our progress forward in life.

We have seen that in this cartoon the verbally evoked target concept of REAL WORRIES is creatively elaborated in the pictorial mode. Crucially, the affordances of the pictorial mode allow for a simultaneous coding of a number of interrelated aspects of the EMOTION frame of REAL WORRIES—the accompanying feeling of sadness, emotional burden, and difficulties in overcoming the state of real worries as well as the force-dynamic causal link between the feeling/experiencing of real worries (the cause) and sadness (the effect). The cartoon thus gives a kind of summary scanning—a snap shot of the emotional experience which in the verbal mode alone would require telling a far longer story.

Of the whole range of metaphors that underlie the meaning of the aphorism in Example 2.9, the creative elaboration of the conventional metaphor EMOTIONAL STATES ARE OBJECTS in terms of which the specific target concept of REAL WORRIES is understood has the highest level of activation on account of its verbo-pictorial construction (and thus, the metaphor REAL WORRIES ARE OBJECTS qualifies as waking). The remaining metaphors, namely: INTENSITY OF AN EMOTIONAL STATE IS THE SIZE OF THE CONTAINER, BODY IS THE CONTAINER FOR EMOTIONS, EMOTIONAL DIFFICULTIES ARE IMPEDIMENTS TO MOTION, EMOTIONAL DIFFICULTIES ARE BURDENS, SADNESS IS A BURDEN, and SAD IS DOWN have only pictorial cues for their activation, hence they would qualify as sleeping. Still, given the frame of REAL WORRIES and, with the focal attention attributed to this emotion in the verbal aphorism, they seem likely to be activated as part of the novel understanding of the target concept in question.

The last cartoon in this study gives an intriguing verbo-pictorial riddle that the addressee is invited to solve to get a novel understanding of two highly elusive EMOTION concepts—HOPE and DESPAIR, whose pictorial rendering would, at face value, seem almost an impossible task to accomplish. To see how the two modalities interact, let us first consider the text. Relying on EMOTIONS ARE FORCES, which, let us recall, Kövecses characterizes as "a single master metaphor for emotion" (2008b, 385), the verbal aphorism portrays HOPE and DESPAIR by means of two causative verbs, respectively, *poszerzać* 'to make sth wider/widen' and *zawężać* 'to make sth narrower/to narrow down', which in their basic senses, refer to physical space. Crucially, the text does not mention any object nominal that would help in identifying what it is that the two actions cause to change, hence it is the pictorial mode that is meant to fill in this syntactic slot.[17] In the drawing, however, there is nothing that would give an easy answer to this query; on their own, the two identical cone-like shapes are, beyond doubt, ambiguous. Still, their location with respect to the protagonist and their contrasting black-white colour are, as

NADZIEJA POSZERZA, ROZPACZ ZAWĘŻA

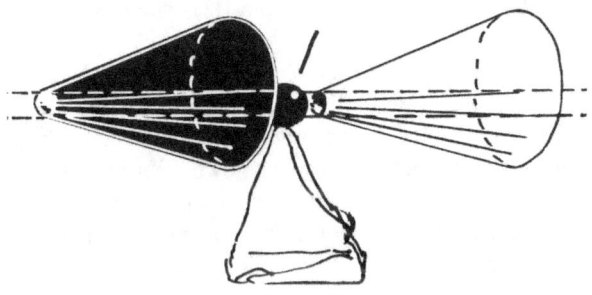

Example 2.10 "*Nadzieja poszerza, rozpacz zawęża*"—'Hope opens (sth) up, despair closes (sth) down (lit. hope makes (it) wider, despair makes (it) narrower)'

Source: Kapusta (2014, 53).

I would like to argue, well-grounded in our conventional patterns of thought. In particular, they may open up the inferencing processes in terms of two conventional metaphors: VISUAL FIELDS ARE CONTAINERS (Lakoff and Johnson 1980, 30) and KNOWING IS SEEING (Sweetser 1990, 37–40). In the context of the verbal aphorism, the cone-like shape located in the line of sight of the protagonist may be interpreted as a visual field whose scope is widened by the emotion of hope.[18] In accord with this construal, the two straight broken lines inside the cone that represents the visual field are an integral part of the pictorial cueing of SEEING as the source domain of the KNOWING IS SEEING metaphor. Analogously to how they are characterized in comics, which is another static visual genre, the two lines inside the cone may be taken to represent lines depicting vision, which, as "highly conventionalized versions of arrows" (Cohn 2013, 38, qtd. in Szawerna 2017, 237), draw the addressee's attention to the directionality of the perceptual experience.[19] Consistent with this construal is the white colour of the cone: in the cognition reading of the verbo-pictorial aphorism on HOPE, it gives grounds for activating one of the entailments of the KNOWING IS SEEING metaphor: good ambient light in the visual field means that one can "see" better, both perceptually and metaphorically. And, if we interpret the black cone that is located at the back of the protagonist's head along the same lines, we may arrive at a contrasting understanding of DESPAIR as an emotion that causes the scope of our visual and cognitive capacities to narrow down. Note, finally, that the colour contrast

44 A Multimodal Case Study of EMOTION Concepts

in the pictorial rendering of the two emotions also invites the opposite axiological assessment of hope and despair as, respectively, positive/good and negative/bad emotional experience. However subtle, this aspect of the verbo-pictorial characterization of HOPE and DESPAIR would be well-motivated by the conventional metaphor GOOD IS LIGHT and its entailment BAD IS DARK or DARKNESS, (see Chapter 1, note 25, and Example 1.2), which are well-established in our culture.[20]

There is yet another aspect of the pictorial rendering of HOPE and DESPAIR in Example 2.10 which may motivate establishing a cohesive tie between the two modes: with respect to the protagonist, the cone in front is widening, while the one at the back is narrowing down, hence the two shapes—via the RESULT FOR ACTION metonymy—may function as metonymic vehicles for accessing the actions expressed by the verbs *poszerzać* 'widen' and *zawężać* 'narrow down'. On this construal, then, the verbo-pictorial elaboration of EMOTIONS ARE FORCES that may serve to motivate the meaning of this aphorism, namely HOPE AND DESPAIR ARE FORCES, would qualify as waking. In turn, the metaphors in terms of which we can come up with an understanding of the effects that these two emotional states may cause (i.e. VISUAL FIELDS ARE CONTAINERS and KNOWING IS SEEING) are all implicit in the pictorial mode only, and so they would qualify as sleeping. To a careful observer, however, they may provide a solution to this conceptual riddle, and thus a novel understanding of the two EMOTION concepts.

2.3 Conclusions

Revealing a complex interplay of the two modes, Janusz Kapusta's verbo-pictorial aphorisms discussed in this study provide supportive evidence for numerous image-schematic metaphors in terms of which EMOTION concepts are understood on an everyday basis. In a number of cases, we have seen that the creative "reworking" of such conventional metaphorical patterns that have served to account for the meaning of the aphorisms resorts to mechanisms that are well-known in verbal forms of expression, namely elaboration as well as extension of conventional mappings and combination of well-entrenched metaphors in one communicative act (for elaborations, see Examples 2.5, 2.9, 2.10; for extension—Example 2.3; and combination—Examples 2.3, 2.6, 2.7, 2.9, 2.10).[21] Still, going beyond a purely verbal "reworking" and providing verbo-pictorial means of expression for grasping the highly elusive nature of abstract EMOTION concepts, both general ones—EMOTION and FEELING, and more specific—LOVE, PAIN, HAPPINESS, UNHAPPINESS, LONELINESS, WORRIES, DESPAIR, and HOPE, Janusz Kapusta's cartoons give a highly original and memorable image of our everyday understanding of emotional experience.

Their spectacular condensation of meaning derives from the affordances of the pictorial mode that allow for a simultaneous expression of diverse aspects of EMOTION concepts. This, let us add, in the sequential mode of purely verbal expression would not be possible. On several occasions, we have seen that conventional metonymies (such as INSTRUMENT FOR ACTION, STAGE OF AN ACTION FOR THE ACTION, SUBEVENT FOR THE EVENT) play a key role in "overcoming" the static nature of this genre.

And more generally, since the discussed metaphors and metonymies have been cued not only in the verbal mode, but also pictorially as well as multimodally, the study strengthens the cognitive assumption on the domain-independent nature of conceptual metaphor and metonymy. The diverse interplay of the two modes reveals that the level of activation of conceptual mechanisms that underlie a coherent interpretation of Janusz Kapusta's aphorisms may vary, ranging from a relatively low activation in the case of their monomodal cueing to a much higher activation level in the case of simultaneous cueing in the two modes. In the dynamic view of metaphor, higher levels of metaphoricity imply that a particular metaphorical construal is attention grabbing and thereby in focal prominence of the discourse. In terms of multimodal rhetoric,[22] they are thus more likely to persuade the addressee to a particular viewpoint that a given verbo-pictorial aphorism invites us to adopt (as in the case of Example 2.2, where a distant perspective to our emotional relationships is taken), or to a particular novel understanding of some EMOTION concept, as in the case of Example 2.8, where a novel understanding of HAPPINESS and of UNHAPPINESS have a high level of metaphoricity on account of their multimodal construction. It was argued, however, that aside from the observable metaphoricity indicators, the specificity of the genre may contribute to increasing the metaphoric quality of a message in which the implicit target concept (cf. the idea of EMOTIONAL DISTANCE in Example 2.1) may be evoked as the focal theme of the aphorisms only due to the interplay of the verbal and pictorial cues which, as is typical of cartoons as a genre, are to be integrated into one coherent message. We have also seen that the incongruity between the pictorial and the verbal construal (of the force-dynamic encounter of individuals in Example 2.3), when integrated into one communicative act, may give rise to humorous effects.

Notes

1. For an illustration of verbo-gestural expression of EMOTION concepts, see, e.g., Müller's discussion of an example of a German speaker who, when characterizing her romantic relationship, performs the "clingy gesture" with the open palms repeatedly touching each other before she produces the verbal metaphor *klebrig* 'clingy' during its production and immediately after (Müller 2008a, 100–101).

2. For an overview of research on intricate relations between gesture and speech, see Müller et al. (2013).
3. According to Kövecses, the other general metonymy in this domain—CAUSE OF EMOTION FOR EMOTION—is less common (2014, 17).
4. For more on this topic, see Kövecses (2000, 2014, 2015b) and also, e.g., Peréz-Rull (2001). For the notion of "highlighting" of aspects of a metaphorical target concept, see, e.g., Kövecses (2002, chap. 7).
5. Arguably, this force-dynamic interaction could also be analysed in terms of the inferences that we draw from the logic of two force schemas—ATTRACTION and COMPULSION (for the latter see Johnson 1987, 45, 47–48; 2007, 137; and Talmy 1988; see also section 1.1.1).
6. The metonymy (REPRESENTATIVE) STAGE OF AN ACTION FOR THE ACTION is a more specific version of SUBEVENT FOR THE EVENT; for the latter see Thornburg and Panther (1997), Kövecses and Radden (1998).
7. Note that the mechanism of "questioning" of the validity or adequacy of a conventional mapping, as Lakoff and Turner (1989, 69–70) show, is characteristic of the poetic use of language.
   In turn, for a cognitive account of incongruity resolution as a source of humorous effects in verbo-visual discourse, see, e.g., Brône and Feyaerts (2004).
8. The gravitational force formula, also known as Newton's Law of Gravitation, defines the magnitude of the force between any two objects as: $Fg = \frac{G \, m_1 \, m_2}{r^2}$, where Fg = gravitational force between two objects; G = gravitational constant; m_1 = mass of the first object (kg); m_2 = mass of the second object (kg); r = distance between objects.
9. For an analysis of Examples 2.7, 2.8, and 2.9 from the perspective of spatialization of abstract thought, see also Górska (in press/2019).
10. For the profile of the analogous English preposition *in*, see, e.g., Langacker (2008, 101–102).
11. For more on image schema clusters, see section 1.1.1.
12. The GRASP schema was first postulated by Chilton (2009).
13. Recall that the different wordings of this metaphor, a.k.a. STATES ARE BOUNDED SPACES (LOCATIONS), reflect different labels of its image-schematic source, which is referred to as the BOUNDED SPACE (LOCATION) or the CONTAINER schema.
14. For more on interrelations between the specific metonymy DOWNWARD BODILY ORIENTATION FOR SADNESS and the SAD IS DOWN metaphor, see Kövecses (2014, 19–20).
15. In CMT, aside from central or constituent mappings (such as STATES ARE CONTAINERS), conceptual metaphors are also characterized in terms of "metaphorical entailments", which refer to the mapping of additional knowledge about a source domain onto a target domain (see Kövecses 2002, chap. 8). Importantly, "[e]ach source concept has a metaphorical entailment potential; that is, it can potentially map extensive everyday knowledge onto the target. We call this everyday knowledge a folk theory or folk understanding of a domain" (Kövecses 2002, 104). In the presently considered example, the entailment is based on our knowledge about the size of containers.
16. For more on the EMOTION frame, see, e.g. Kövecses (2014, 23).
17. The phenomenon of filling in a syntactic slot by means of a gestural expression is well known in gesture studies; see, e.g., Müller and Cienki (2009, 304); Müller and Tag (2010); Müller, Ladewig, and Bressem (2013, 65–66); and Ladewig (2014) and the literature cited therein.

18. For an extensive discussion of metaphorization of VISUAL FIELDS as CONTAINERS in comics, see Szawerna (2017, 157–166).
19. For more on the role of "visual vectors [that] result whenever there are explicit or implicit 'lines' created by visual forms in an image" in dynamic interpretations of static visuals (such as painting and picture books), see Bateman (2014, 59–60).
20. The constitutive role of the source domain of DARKNESS is also evident in wordless animation films about DEPRESSION that are analysed by Forceville and Paling (2018); the authors argue that DEPRESSION IS A DARK MONSTER and DEPRESSION IS A DARK CONFINING SPACE are two dominant visual metaphors in their data.
21. For more on reworking of conventional metaphors, see, e.g., Lakoff and Turner (1989), Kövecses (2002), Dancygier and Sweetser (2014, 57–59).
22. For more on visual and multimodal rhetoric, see Ortiz (2010), Kjeldsen (2015a,b, 2018), Pollaroli, and Rocci (2015), Hidalgo-Downing and Kraljevic-Mujic (2016), Tseronis and Forceville (2017a,b).

3 A Multimodal Case Study of LIFE

Focusing on the role of image schemas in metaphorical understanding of human life, this case study examines another sample of verbo-pictorial aphorisms by Janusz Kapusta, a Polish artist. Among them, the construal of LIFE as a long-term purposeful activity is by far the most common, and therefore it is not surprising that the PATH image schema and the characteristic affordance of path that is grasped by the MOTION schema provide experiential grounds for understanding diverse aspects of this abstract concept (section 3.1). The less common conceptions are exemplified by a few aphorisms that construe LIFE as A GAME and A SHOW (section 3.2); in these examples, the image-schematic structuring, though foundational, is less evident since it is embedded in culturally elaborate and rich constructs. Except for two examples considered in section 3.3, the analysed multimodal aphorisms are all based on conventional metaphors. It is the "creative reworking" of conventional mappings, in either one mode or across the verbal and the pictorial modes, that accounts for the novelty of the discussed metaphors. In more general terms, this study provides further support to the dynamic theory of metaphor (see section 1.3), since it makes it apparent that the degree of overlap of the elements cued in the two modes varies considerably and, by the same token, activation levels of metaphoric source and target domains turn out to be gradable and dynamic. It is also argued that the novelty of the mapping should be included among the factors that may increase the metaphor's activation level.

3.1 The PATH Schema and the JOURNEY OF LIFE[1]

The PATH schema (a.k.a. SOURCE-PATH-GOAL, see section 1.1.1) is one of the most common source domains on which we rely in our understanding of numerous abstract concepts that are far less immediate in our experience and hence more difficult to grasp. Evidence for such image-schematic metaphorical understanding has been frequently derived from linguistic data alone (see, e.g., Lakoff and Johnson 1980, 1999; Lakoff and Turner 1989; Lakoff 1993).

And so, for example, the fact that we talk about *a clear line of argument, a career path*, and *a cross-roads in a romantic relationship* or *in life* was taken as indicating that we not only talk about the respective metaphorical target domains of ARGUMENT, CAREER, LOVE, and LIFE in terms of the PATH schema, but also reason about them in these terms and behave accordingly. With the advent of multimodal metaphor research (Forceville 1996; Cienki 1998a), it has become evident that the PATH schema, either alone or as a part of an image schema complex (see section 1.1.1), is commonly evoked to provide structuring for metaphorical rendering of abstract concepts in multimodal discourse, including verbo-gestural communication (see, e.g., Kolter et al. 2012) and verbo-visuals, such as advertisements (Yu 2009), comics (Potsch and Williams 2012), editorial cartoons (Abdel-Raheem 2014), documentaries (Forceville 2006, 2011b), and animation films (Forceville and Jeulink 2011; Forceville 2013, 2016a). Following the multimodal line of research, in this section I will focus on the PATH schema in Janusz Kapusta's verbo-pictorial aphorisms on LIFE.

The notion of LIFE in Example 3.1 is not evoked explicitly, yet the activation of the well-entrenched submapping of the conventional conceptual metaphor LIFE IS A JOURNEY, namely LIFE GOALS ARE DESTINATIONS (Lakoff 1993), seems almost inevitable if we want to integrate the verbal and the pictorial mode into a coherent communicative act.

Example 3.1 "*Świat dokądś zmierza, co wcale nie oznacza, że idziemy w tym samym kierunku*"—'The world is heading somewhere, which does not mean that we are going in the same direction'

Source: Kapusta (2014, 179).

Note first that in the pictorial mode the idea of goal-directed motion is evoked metonymically[2] by two directional symbols: a white road sign which, with respect to the protagonist, is oriented forward in the horizontal plane, i.e., in the direction of the canonical human motion, and a road-sign-like black vehicle on which the protagonist sits that points in the opposite direction. In effect, the pictorial mode provides explicit cues for a metonymic activation of the PATH schema on which basic correspondences of the LIFE IS A JOURNEY metaphor are based, of which two primary metaphors (section 1.1.2), PURPOSES ARE DESTINATIONS and ACTION IS MOTION, provide the embodied motivation to the presently considered submapping in terms of which we understand our LIFE GOALS.[3] These two primary metaphors, as Lakoff and Johnson (1999, 60–61) argue, are combined with the cultural belief according to which "[p]eople are supposed to have purposes in life, and they are supposed to act so as to achieve those purposes" (Lakoff and Johnson 1999, 61). Taken together they give rise to "a profoundly influential folk model" in our culture, whose core can be given as "a metaphorical version of that cultural belief: People are supposed to have destinations in life, and they are supposed to move so as to achieve those destinations" (Lakoff and Johnson 1999, 60–61). The submappings that constitute this complex folk model can be stated in the form of the following metaphors:

"A PURPOSEFUL LIFE IS A JOURNEY
A PERSON LIVING A LIFE IS A TRAVELER
LIFE GOALS ARE DESTINATIONS
A LIFE PLAN IS AN ITINERARY".

(Lakoff and Johnson 1999, 61)[4]

But why, one may wonder, the pictorially cued idea of human motion forward towards some destination is likely to evoke this metaphorical folk model in the first place? For one thing, this model provides a motivated link for establishing a cohesive tie between the pictorial and the verbal mode. Specifically, the pictorial cue of the road-sign pointing to the motion forward can be integrated with the idea of the goal directed motion expressed verbally by the verb *idziemy* 'we are going/walking' and the prepositional phrase *w tym samym kierunku* 'in the same direction'. More importantly, in the verbal aphorism the protagonist contrasts his own "human" motion with the motion of the world at large and, in effect, shifts the perspective and turns his statement about his own physical motion towards a destination into a general comment about his pursuit of life goals. In brief, for a coherent interpretation of the cartoon, the metaphorical interpretation of the two objects in motion—the world and the human being—seems inevitable.[5] This considered, we may assume that not only the understanding of the PURPOSEFUL ACTIVITY OF

THE WORLD at large, but also a PROTAGONIST'S LIFE GOALS in terms of MOTION TOWARDS A DESTINATION would qualify as waking metaphors (see Table 1.2), despite the fact that only the target domain of the WORLD'S PURPOSEFUL ACTIVITY is rendered explicit, while that of the PROTAGONIST'S LIFE GOALS is evoked indirectly—by the immediate verbo-pictorial context and cultural beliefs (cf. the folk model of life above). Note that this account, similarly to the analysis of Example 2.1 earlier, rests on the assumption that, in the genre of verbo-pictorial aphorisms, the construction of an abstract target concept that is evoked without any explicit metaphoricity indicators (see section 1.3) may bring the implicit notion into the focal attention of the addressee, and thereby render the metaphor that provides the relevant understanding "awake".

Just like in Example 3.1, in the second cartoon the notion of LIFE is not explicit, yet given the convention of the genre, on the one hand, and the generic statement referring to Everyman that is expressed in the text, on the other hand, this verbo-pictorial aphorism is bound to be interpreted in terms of our conventional understanding of PURPOSEFUL ACTIVITIES AS A JOURNEY, of which the LIFE JOURNEY is, in accordance with the earlier characterized folk model, a prime instance.[6] Similarly to the previous example, a coherent interpretation of the verbo-pictorial aphorism is based on well-entrenched conventional mappings only. In this case, the activation of two conventional metaphors seems crucial; one of them—MAKING CHOICES (IN LIFE) IS MAKING DECISION ABOUT WHICH WAY TO GO—is an entailment of LIFE IS A JOURNEY and the

Example 3.2 "Chociaż mamy nieskończoną ilość dróg do wyboru i tak pójdziemy tylko jedną"— 'Even though we have an infinite number of paths to choose from, we will follow only one'

Source: Kapusta (2014, 302).

other—MEANS ARE PATHS—constitutes a submapping of the LOCATION EVENT-STRUCTURE metaphor (Lakoff and Johnson 1999, 179; see also section 2.2 in this volume). Arguably, the novelty resides here in making the addressee aware that there is an infinite number of paths from which one has to choose a single route to follow. The pictorial mode elaborates this conception by metonymically representing a "route sample", with each route pointing to a slightly different direction. The spatial closeness of the routes in the sample may be interpreted in terms of the SIMILARITY IS CLOSENESS metaphor (see section 1.1.2), which, in turn, may be said to highlight the degree of difficulty of this choice: selecting a single route out of a range of spatially close paths is by no means an easy task. Note, further, that the latter metaphor, on account of being cued in the pictorial mode only, would qualify as sleeping. By contrast, the other two conventional metaphors that take the source domain of PATH would qualify as waking, since the PATH schema is cued multimodally in this cartoon.

Unlike the first two examples, the remaining cartoons that are considered in this section all explicitly evoke the target concept of LIFE, and they are all based on some creative reworking of conventional metaphors, of which extension and elaboration are, as in the case of EMOTION concepts in Chapter 2, most common mechanisms. The former, let us recall (see in particular, section 2.3), resides in mapping of an element of the source domain that is not evoked in the conventional metaphoric understanding of a target concept, while the latter enriches a conventional mapping by rendering it more specific.

Both extension and elaboration of LIFE IS A JOURNEY underlie the meaning construction of the verbo-pictorial aphorism in Example 3.3.

Specifically, by verbally stating that "*W podróży życia wszystkie bilety są w jedną stronę*" 'In the journey of life, all tickets are one-way', the aphorism extends the conventional metaphor in that it evokes—via the metonymic reference point that is cued by the expression *bilety* 'tickets'—the idea of travelling in a vehicle; and it elaborates the conventional mapping by specifying the journey as a one-way trip. In effect, the text highlights the aspect of LIFE that is "hidden" by the conventional metaphor, namely, the idea that every LIFE JOURNEY inevitably ends up in death and there is no return back to life.[7] Note that in this simple way attention is drawn to the core of the cultural model of LIFE that is typical of Western culture which, let us add, contrasts with idea of life-and-rebirth cycles that is characteristic of, e.g., the Buddhist tradition. Pictorially, the idea of a one-way trip is cued metonymically via the conception of PATH (i.e., in terms of the PATH FOR MOTION metonymy) that is depicted as a vector pointing in the direction of the canonical human motion. Note, further, that in the pictorial mode attention is drawn to this novel aspect of the JOURNEY metaphor by the conspicuously large size of the vector, which,

W PODRÓŻY ŻYCIA WSZYSTKIE BILETY SĄ W JEDNĄ STRONĘ

Example 3.3 *"W podróży życia wszystkie bilety są w jedną stronę"*—'In the journey of life, all tickets are one-way'
Source: *Plus Minus*, January 17, 2015.

let us add, is a visual rendition of the primary metaphor IMPORTANT IS BIG. Observe, finally, that, on account of its verbo-pictorial construction, the level of activation of the mapping LIFE JOURNEY IS A ONE WAY TRIP IN A PUBLIC TRANSPORT VEHICLE would qualify as a waking metaphor.

The verbo-pictorial aphorism in Example 3.4 is based on the figure/ground reversal of two elements of the source domain of JOURNEY: the traveller and the landscape. Unlike on physical journeys, where the landscape keeps changing while the traveller stays the same, in this cartoon, on the LIFE JOURNEY evoked verbally, the traveller is conceived as 'the changing landscape' and the very same conception is rendered specific in the pictorial mode. In effect, this aphorism extends the conventional metaphor by adding a novel mapping: THE TRAVELLER IS THE (CHANGING) LANDSCAPE. We may note also that since this mapping is cued multimodally its level of activation is high and, by the same token, the metaphor qualifies as waking.

The LIFE IS A JOURNEY metaphor is also extended in Example 3.5, where the text, by referring to the duration of stopovers (cf. *punkt przestankowy* 'a stopover'), introduces a novel element of the source and maps it onto the target concept of LIFE. This novel mapping provides a basis for an alternative construal of the LIFE JOURNEY itself—the one in which breaks in a journey may last longer than the journey as a whole. Entailments of this metaphorical construal are noteworthy: the traveller whose stopovers last longer than his whole journey does not seem to have a clear itinerary and,

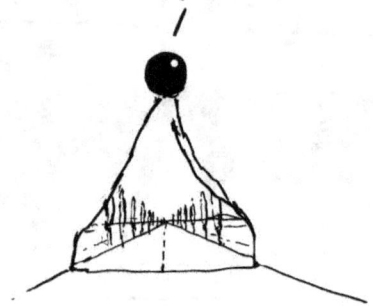

Example 3.4 "*W podróży przez życie to my sami jesteśmy zmieniającym się krajobrazem*"—'In the journey through life, it's us who are the changing landscape'

Source: Kapusta (2014, 76).

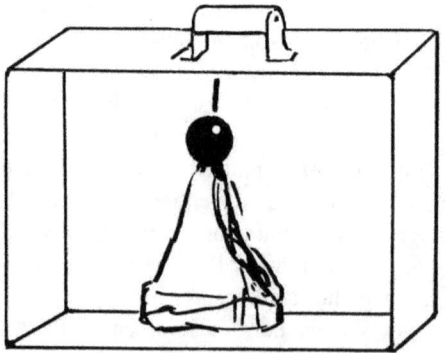

Example 3.5 "*W życiu punkty przestankowe mogą być dłuższe niż podróż*"—'In life stopovers may be longer than the journey'

Source: Kapusta (2014, 229).

therefore, is unlikely to reach his destination; this entails the traveller not acting in accordance with the dominant cultural model in terms of which we are expected to follow a life plan and aim at achieving our life goals (cf. the folk model of life above). The pictorial mode seems to strengthen this interpretation. In particular, we may establish here a cohesive tie between the verbally evoked idea of the traveller staying at a stopover and the image of the protagonist who is depicted in the drawing as wholly contained within a huge suitcase. It needs to be noted that, in the pictorial mode, the suitcase functions as a "double" metonymic vehicle in that it provides mental access, on the one hand, to the JOURNEY domain and, on the other hand, to the source domain of the primary metaphor STATES ARE LOCATIONS/CONTAINERS/BOUNDED SPACES.[8] Being stuck within a single location that is pictorially cued as the suitcase and verbally as the prolonged duration of (the STATE of) a stopover, the protagonist is, of course, not making any progress (cf. PROGRESS IS MOTION FORWARD, Lakoff 1993) so as to achieve his life goals. It may be argued, further, that the pictorial mode opens up another aspect of this "non-agentive" construal of the LIFE JOURNEY: the protagonist, rather than carrying a suitcase himself, is being passively carried on in it by some unspecified agentive force. Whether this image of the protagonist being carried on in time is to be interpreted as positive, negative, or just as an ironic comment on life is left open.

As for the metaphoricity level, in this cartoon the idea of STATES AS LOCATIONS is evoked both verbally (cf. the expression *punkty przestankowe* 'stopovers') and pictorially (by the image of the suitcase "containing" the protagonist), hence the metaphor's activation is high (and the metaphor qualifies as waking). Likewise, we have both verbal and pictorial indexes of the source domain of LIFE IS A JOURNEY, hence this metaphor has a high activation level. In turn, the concept of the prolonged duration of stopovers relative to that of the length of the journey as a whole is explicitly cued in the verbal mode only; however, on account of its novelty, the mapping of this conception onto the domain of LIFE is bound to draw the addressee's attention. This, in turn, implies that the level of metaphoricity is high and the creative metaphor should be characterized as "awake". In more general terms, this analysis indicates that the level of metaphoricity cannot be established as a simple measure of the "observable metaphoricity indicators" (see section 1.3) and that, on account of its attention-drawing effects, the novelty of a mapping should be regarded as one of the factors that increase the level of metaphoricity.

Yet another creative extension of LIFE IS A JOURNEY constitutes the "gist" of the verbo-pictorial aphorism in Example 3.6. Note first that the PATH schema is cued in the pictorial mode only—the drawing depicts it as a line formed by a series of four figural shapes of decreasing size. We can, however,

Example 3.6 "*Przemijamy przez całe życie, ale pod koniec jakby bardziej*"—'We are passing throughout the whole life but, when close to the end, as if a bit more'

Source: Kapusta (2014, 70).

establish a cohesive tie between the pictorial conception of PATH and the verbally expressed idea of our passing throughout our life-span, with the verb *przemijać* 'elapse, pass, go by (in time)'[9] providing access to the MOVING EGO model of TIME, and thereby to the MOTION schema which lies at its core. Since the correlation of the PATH and MOTION schemas recurs regularly in our embodied experience, the interpretation of the cartoon in terms of this cross-modal cohesive tie seems natural and well-motivated. Integration of this conception with the second clause crucially relies on a cross-modal activation of the SCALE schema: the verbal mode specifies that the intensity of 'our passing throughout the life-span' increases along some scale, and the pictorial mode, relying on the UP-DOWN and BIG-SMALL schemas, depicts this intensity scale in terms of the protagonist's dramatic change in form and size along the vertical dimension. For our purpose, the creative multimodal metaphor which underlies this interpretation can be phrased as: PASSING IN LIFE IS MOTION FORWARD ALONG A HORIZONTAL PATH COINCIDING WITH THE MOTION DOWNWARD ALONG THE VERTICAL PATH OF AN EGO DISAPPEARING IN THE GROUND. Importantly, the embodied inferential structure of the UP-DOWN and BIG-SMALL schemas triggers the assignment of axiological values to the intensity scale—with its endpoints—the initial state of 'being up and big' (hence active, important, and in the peak of power)[10] evaluated as positive, and the final state of 'the reduced body being down—almost completely submerged in the ground' (hence, unable to act, unimportant, and powerless)—as negative.[11]

We may observe, further, that the activation level of the presently considered metaphor qualifies as high for a number of reasons: aside from the novelty of the mapping, there are also multiple verbal and/or pictorial cues that evoke its conceptual core—the idea of self-propelled motion forward that provides structure both to the LIFE JOURNEY metaphor and to the MOVING EGO MODEL OF TIME. Likewise, the idea of the intensity of our PASSING IN LIFE is highly salient, since we have both the verbal and the pictorial cues evoking the conception of SCALE.

In the last aphorism considered in this section, the cartoon's protagonist dwells upon life in general, yet given the visual arrangement of the drawing, with the centrally positioned protagonist who is encircled by a bounded "path", the conception of human life understood in the terms of the PATH schema comes to the fore. Specifically, the cartoon can be interpreted as a creative reworking of two metaphors of LIFE—LIFE IS A JOURNEY and LIFE IS LIGHT, which are combined with the metaphor KNOWING IS SEEING. Both target concepts—LIFE and AWARENESS—are expressed verbally (cf. *życie* 'life', *świadome* 'aware'), while the respective source domains are cued multimodally. The source domain of the JOURNEY metaphor is verbally characterized as a motion of a liquid along a path, which is expressed by means of the noun *fontanna* 'fountain', two motion verbs, *wynurzać się* 'emerge' and *powracać* 'come back', which are accompanied by the path prepositions *z* 'from' and *do* 'to'. Pictorially, the

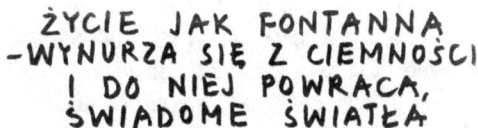

Example 3.7 "*Życie jak fontanna—wynurza się z ciemności i do niej powraca, świadome światła*"—'Life like a fountain—emerges from the darkness and comes back to it, having become aware of light'

Source: Kapusta (2014, 258).

corresponding path of motion is visualized as a fountain-like beam of light which increases in size and changes in colour from dark to white, gradually encircling the protagonist and, with respect to him, heading from the back towards the front (the directionality is indicated by the fountain's increasing size and the endpoint of motion is indicated by the circles which spread out from the fountain on the dark surface at the bottom).[12]

Note, finally, that in this cartoon there is a very high degree of overlap in the multimodal activation of the source domain of JOURNEY, since the cluster of the PATH, MOTION, and BOUNDEDNESS schemas is cued in both modes.[13] Likewise, the source domain of the metaphoric understanding of AWARENESS, namely LIGHT, is also cued multimodally (cf. the noun *światło* 'light' and the whiteness of the fountain intensified as it approaches the black surface). By contrast, the LIFE IS LIGHT metaphor is not explicitly cued verbally and, therefore, this conventional metaphor would be qualified as sleeping. But, given the context of the verbal aphorism whose explicit topic is LIFE, on the one hand, and the pictorial representation of the fountain in the form of a beam of light, on the other hand, it stands a good chance of becoming "awake" for some recipients and thus enriching their interpretation of this cartoon.

3.2 LIFE AS A GAME and A SHOW

As compared to the dominant multimodal renderings of LIFE IS A JOURNEY, in his verbo-pictorial aphorisms on LIFE Janusz Kapusta resorts to other conventional metaphors only sporadically. Two such metaphors—LIFE IS A GAME and LIFE IS A SHOW or ENTERTAINMENT (Kövecses 2005, 84–86; 184–189)—motivate the meaning of cartoons that are considered in this section. Both source domains—GAME and SHOW/ENTERTAINMENT—evoke culturally rich and well-structured bodies of knowledge, hence they provide good grounds for the reworking of these conventional metaphors in novel ways.

The aphorisms in Examples 3.8 and 3.9 both rework the correspondence of LIFE IS A GAME which may be regarded as the "central mapping" of this metaphor, which grasps our understanding of SUCCESS and FAILURE IN LIFE in terms of WINNING and LOSING IN A GAME.[14] Importantly, they both rely on the mechanism that we have encountered only once so far (see Example 2.4), namely the "questioning" of the validity or adequacy of a conventional mapping (see note 7, Chapter 2).

To analyse Example 3.8, let us first consider the verbal aphorism, which elaborates the LIFE IS A GAME metaphor by specifying the source domain as an Olympic game, and characterizes the understanding of success in life in terms of this specific game as inadequate by stating that: 'Life

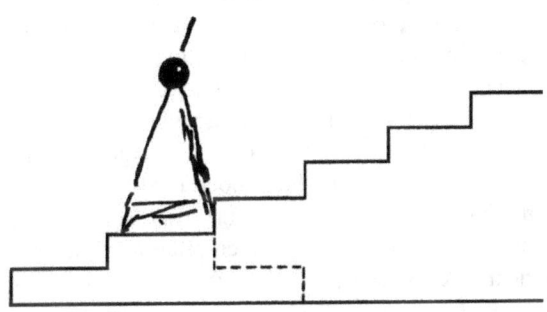

Example 3.8 "*Życie nie jest olimpiadą. Przyznaje o wiele więcej nagród niż trzy medale*"—'Life is not an Olympic competition. It gives many more awards than three medals'

Source: *Plus Minus*, August 6, 2016.

is not an Olympic competition. It gives many more awards than three medals'. Clearly, in the verbal mode, LIFE is portrayed as a PERSON; this conception rests on the image-schematic metaphors ABSTRACT IDEAS ARE OBJECTS (PERSONS) and CAUSES ARE FORCES as well as on the metaphorical understanding of EVENTS AS ACTIONS, which, taken together, motivate the construal of successful events as the result of some causal wilful action of an agent—the "giver"—and of those who succeed in life as passive recipients of awards.

Unsurprisingly, the image-schematic structuring expressed in the pictorial mode relies on the UP-DOWN schema as the experiential base for understanding SUCCESS (cf. SUCCESS IS UP): the drawing depicts the protagonist on what may be readily interpreted as the location of a person awarded the gold medal in an Olympic competition, and portrays the verbally evoked possibility of receiving many more medals by the image of steps leading upwards. On account of its multimodal construction, the level of activation of this mapping qualifies the metaphor SUCCESS IS UP as waking. The same applies to the multimodally "reworked" metaphor LIFE IS A GAME where, we should add, by questioning the adequacy of the elaborated version of this metaphor, the aphorism draws the focal attention to the negated understanding of LIFE.

60 A Multimodal Case Study of LIFE

Unlike Example 3.8, in the next cartoon the verbal aphorism evokes a general concept of GAME and questions the validity of the conventional understanding of LIFE in these terms by stating that in the game of life 'the winner always loses'.

The pictorial mode ingeniously elaborates the verbal message: the depicted protagonist can be interpreted as a winner and a loser at the same time. Specifically, his position on the level of a higher platform cues his construal as a winner (via SUCCESS IS UP), however the fact that he is depicted as having no supporting ground implies that he is just about to fall down into some vast space below him; when mapped onto the target domain of LIFE, this image portrays him as a person who is bound to be a loser. Crucially, it is the logic of the image-schema cluster of UP-DOWN, FORCE, SUPPORT, BALANCE, and MOTION that underlies the dynamic interpretation of the drawing. Relying on our experiential knowledge, we can evoke (via STAGE OF AN ACTION FOR THE ACTION) the metonymically cued scenario of FALLING DOWN: without supporting ground, the force of gravity will cause the protagonist to change his current state of being up and make him fall down. Observe that this interpretation of the drawing is motivated by two primary metaphors, namely STATES ARE LOCATIONS[15] and CHANGE OF STATE IS A CHANGE OF LOCATION. And it is these metaphors, in combination with the metaphor SUCCESS IS UP and its entailment LOSING SUCCESS IS FALLING DOWN, that provide a novel understanding of SUCCESS and FAILURE that is the main theme of this verbo-pictorial aphorism on LIFE. And as in the previous example, on account of the multimodal construction,

Example 3.9 *"Życie jest grą, w której zwycięzca zawsze przegrywa"*—'Life is a game in which the winner always loses'

Source: *Plus Minus*, April 21, 2018.

the level of activation of the creatively reworked metaphors LIFE IS A GAME as well as SUCCESS IS UP and LOSING SUCCESS IS FALLING DOWN qualifies these metaphors as waking. Moreover, considering the span of human life as a whole, the aphorism portrays the endpoint of human life as an inevitable failure and, when viewed from this perspective, success in life turns out to be temporary and insignificant. Arguably, the novelty of this construal of LIFE IS A GAME is likely to contribute to the metaphoricity of this verbo-pictorial aphorism.

The conventional metaphor, which underlies the meaning of the aphorism in Example 3.10, in the literature on the subject was analysed at two different levels of generality: at the general level, as LIFE IS A SHOW or ENTERTAINMENT (Kövecses 2005, 184–189) and, at a more specific level, as LIFE IS A (THEATRE) PLAY (Lakoff and Turner 1989, 20–23; Kövecses 2005). In terms of the terminology that we already know, we can say that the latter metaphor "elaborates" or "instantiates" the former, more general metaphor. Note now, that the verbal aphorism in Example 3.10, by stating that '[i]n the theatre of life everybody plays the main part', provides explicit linguistic cues for activating the more specific version of the conventional metaphor and renders it still more specific by narrowing down the source domain to a theatre play by a single actor, hence a monodrama.

As in Example 3.9, the interplay of the metaphor STATES ARE LOCATIONS and the metonymy STAGE OF AN ACTION FOR THE ACTION provides grounds, on the one hand, for establishing cohesive ties between the text and the drawing and, on the other hand, for the drawing's dynamic interpretation (cf. THEATRE STAGE

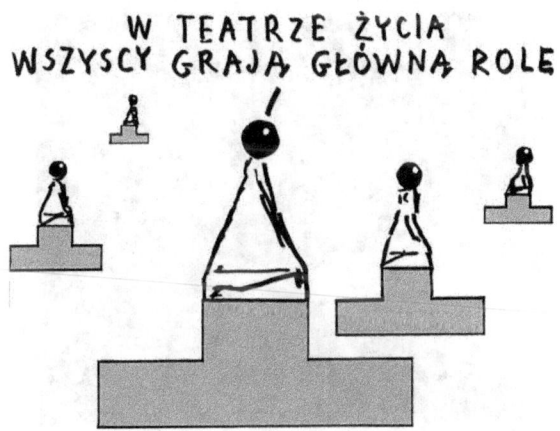

Example 3.10 "*W teatrze życia wszyscy grają główną rolę*"—'In the theatre of life everybody plays the main part'

Source: *Plus Minus*, March 5, 2011.

FOR PLAYING [ON THAT STAGE]). Moreover, by depicting the figures on platforms on which there is space for only one individual, the drawing strengthens the verbally evoked conception of a theatre play in which all actors play the main part. As for the image-schematic structuring, the drawing, aside from the BOUNDED SPACE schema (which, as was already noted, provides experiential ground for the conception of STATES AS LOCATIONS), in depicting the figures on the elevated platforms cues the activation of the UP-DOWN schema as the source domain for the metaphor IMPORTANT/SIGNIFICANT IS UP, and thereby opens up a motivated link with the verbal characterization of actors playing the main part (it can be rendered as THE MAIN PART IN A PLAY IS UP). As for the metaphoricity level, this conception of THE MAIN PART is verbally explicit and cued pictorially, hence its multimodal expression qualifies as a waking metaphor. Likewise, the multimodal construal of LIFE IS A THEATRE PLAY assigns the focal prominence to this metaphor, and thereby renders it "awake".

The verbo-pictorial aphorism in Example 3.11 can also be analysed at two different levels of generality: at the general level, as LIFE IS A SHOW/ENTERTAINMENT and at a more specific level, as LIFE IS A MOVIE. In this case, however, in the literature on the subject, the more specific version of the metaphor is characterized as a novel elaboration of the general conventional pattern LIFE IS A SHOW/ENTERTAINMENT (Benczes and Ságvári 2018, 136).[16] Unlike in the examples discussed so far in this section, where the main theme was the individual's success or role in life, in this example the evaluation of events as they unfold in the course of one's life is at issue. Similarly to any other kind

Example 3.11 "*Film zwany życiem potrzebuje i światła i ciemności*"—'The film called life needs both light and darkness'

Source: Kapusta (2014, 13).

of sequential narrative telling a story (e.g., a myth or a novel), the verbally evoked concept of MOVIE (cf. the expression film 'a movie') is an excellent source domain for highlighting this aspect of LIFE. Moreover, evoking rich well-structured knowledge that is common to the general public at large, the MOVIE domain is well-suited for drawing entailments. At the same time, however, a provision should be made for a wide margin of individual differences in the inferencing process based on this metaphor since the people's knowledge of this domain will also depend on their age as well as the cultural and social background.

As is characteristic of this genre, in this cartoon the target concept is evoked verbally, while the source domain of MOVIE is cued by verbo-pictorial means. The drawing depicts what can be easily recognized as a cinema-hall, with the protagonist surrounded by the darkness of a screening room and the white cone-like shape at the line of his sight representing the light emitted from the operating cine-camera. We can thus say that the black-white contrast in the drawing performs a metonymic function in that via ATTRIBUTE FOR OBJECT/THING (HAVING THAT ATTRIBUTE) it provides mental access—a metonymic shortcut—to the two characteristic elements of the experience of watching a movie in a cinema-hall.

Crucially, within the MOVIE domain itself, the black-white contrast of the drawing and the verbally expressed concepts of LIGHT and DARKNESS (cf., respectively, the expressions *światło* 'light' and *ciemność* 'darkness') may also be interpreted metaphorically in terms of the LIGHT-DARK image schema (a.k.a. BRIGHT-DARK) which motivates the well-established patterns: GOOD IS LIGHT/BAD IS DARK and HAPPY IS LIGHT/SAD IS DARK. Following Ortiz (2011, 1571–1572, 2014), we may add at this point that, in film-making, it is commonplace to use shadows and various lighting effects as visual metaphors and, as the author argues, the expressive success of such *mise-en-scène* techniques lies in their rooting in the primary metaphors GOOD IS LIGHT/BAD IS DARK and HAPPY IS LIGHT /SAD IS DARK.[17] This observation also applies to how the LIGHT-DARK image schema was creatively employed to portray the state of DEPRESSION by purely visual means in short wordless animation films studied by Forceville and Paling (2018). Moreover, in the genre of film as a whole, this source domain may provide experiential grounds for a metaphorical understanding of a number of abstract concepts which need not be cued explicitly to be inferred by some attentive viewers (Forceville and Renckens 2013). Aside from the already mentioned GOOD/BAD and HAPPY/SAD, the concepts of KNOWLEDGE/IGNORANCE are commonly understood in terms of this domain. And, more precisely, KNOWLEDGE IS LIGHT and IGNORANCE IS DARKNESS are metaphorical correspondences that are entailed by the dominant conventional pattern in our culture, namely KNOWING IS SEEING (Sweetser 1990);[18] experientially, good, ambient light provides good conditions for seeing better perceptually, which, in terms of this metaphor, entails better knowledge; and by implication, from visual darkness we can infer poor knowledge and ignorance. In effect, in the medium of film, various techniques which rely on the LIGHT-DARK schema are likely to bring ambiguity in meaning that prompts creative and aesthetically pleasing interpretations (Forceville and Renckens 2013, 164). When considered in the context of Example 3.11, this aspect of the source domain of MOVIE may serve to highlight different aspects of LIFE and thereby enrich the individual, more specific interpretations of this verbo-pictorial aphorism. In terms of the dynamic theory of metaphor (see section 1.3, and Table 1.2), however, since none of the potential target concepts—GOOD/BAD, HAPPY/SAD, and KNOWLEDGE/IGNORANCE—is explicit in this aphorism, the level of activation of image-schematic metaphors that could highlight aspects of these concepts in terms of LIGHT-DARK is low, hence they should be classified as sleeping. Recall, however, that in the revised approach that I advocate here, the specificity of the genre may contribute to the activation level of a metaphor whose target domain is only implicit (see the analysis of Examples 2.1, 2.2, 3.1, and 3.2). In particular, the verbo-pictorial aphorisms are a kind of conceptual riddle in which the message conveyed across two different modes should be integrated into one coherent communicative act. If we analyse Example 3.11 from this perspective, we can say that whenever the addressee considers the explicitly evoked concepts of LIFE and MOVIE in terms of any of the previously mentioned image-schematic metaphors with the LIGHT-DARK source domain, he brings them into his focal attention, and thereby renders them "awake". Still, when we stay at the general level of LIFE IS A MOVIE, we should say that, from the perspective of the original version of the dynamic theory, the presence of the verbal and the pictorial indicators of the LIGHT-DARK schema qualifies the activation level of this metaphor as high and the metaphor itself as waking.

3.3 LIFE and the Domains of PAINTING and SOUND

Truly novel, creative metaphors are a rarity, which is not surprising, since, as Lakoff and Johnson observe in their seminal work, "it is by no means an easy matter to change the metaphors we live by" (1980, 145). For the present purpose of analysing Janusz Kapusta's verbo-pictorial aphorisms on LIFE which are based on source domains that are not evoked in our conventional understanding of this concept, it is important to note that, in CMT, description of such metaphors resorts to the same tools that are used to analyse conventional metaphors, of which metaphorical entailments and the highlighting of aspects of a target concept are directly relevant to our present concern.

Taking a distant view on LIFE, the verbal aphorism in Example 3.12 evokes a very rich cultural domain of PAINTING and construes the course of an individual life in terms of the process of painting on canvas, the final outcome

ŻYCIE JEST JAK PŁÓTNO MALARSKIE.
JEDEN NAMALUJE NA NIM ARCYDZIEŁO,
DRUGI TANDETNY OBRAZ

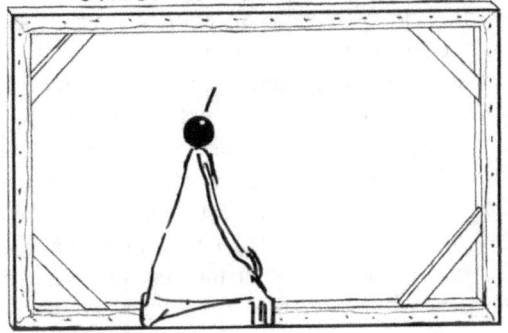

Example 3.12 "*Życie jest jak płótno malarskie. Jeden namaluje na nim arcydzieło, drugi tandetny obraz*"—'Life is like a canvas. One will paint a masterpiece on it, another—a shoddy/cheap picture'

Source: *Plus Minus*, August 12, 2017.

of which may turn out to be either a masterpiece or a shoddy/cheap picture. Note now that the pictorial mode establishes a cohesive tie with the key element of the verbal aphorism that is expressed as *płótno malarskie* 'painting canvas'—in the drawing, the protagonist is depicted as standing in front of a huge framed unpainted canvas. Relying on the vast entailment potential of this source domain (see note 12, Chapter 2), the addressees may recruit a lot of additional knowledge to highlight particular aspects of LIFE; however, the range and the level of specificity of metaphorical entailments would, to a large extent, be a matter of the person's individual experience and aesthetic values. Still, certain aspects of the PAINTING domain are commonly shared by the general public at large, and they may give rise to some shared understanding of LIFE in terms of the novel metaphor that underlies the meaning of this aphorism. The common entailments would include the mappings, such as: LIFE IS A PIECE OF ART; THE PERSON LIVING A LIFE IS A PAINTER; LIVING A LIFE IS A CREATIVE PROCESS. They may serve to highlight, e.g.: the idea that, just like any piece of art, an individual's life will be evaluated by others; just like a painter is responsible for whether he creates a masterpiece or a cheap picture, the individual is responsible for whether his life is beautiful and aesthetically pleasing or ugly.

As for the image-schematic structuring of Example 3.12, the cluster of the OBJECT and the BOUNDED SPACE schemas lies at the core of the source domain of PAINTING CANVAS in terms of which the target concept of LIFE is understood in this aphorism. Note, finally, that the level of activation of this metaphor is high for two reasons. On the one hand, there is a high overlap in the conceptual content of the verbal and pictorial cueing of the source domain. And on the other hand, the comparative adverb *jak* 'like' prompts the construction of a multimodal simile and, by drawing attention to the metaphoric quality of the aphorism, it also contributes to a higher activation level of the metaphor.

The last aphorism in my data sample resorts to the source domain of SOUND which, as has been already indicated, is not conventionally evoked in the metaphors of LIFE. Relying on our common knowledge that a single sound's endurance in time is momentary, it draws an explicit comparison (cf. the adverb *jak* 'like') between the temporal boundedness of a human life and of a physical sound, which can be stated as a novel metaphor THE TIMESPAN OF A HUMAN LIFE IS THE DURATION OF A SOUND. In this very simple and ingenious way, the verbal aphorism highlights an aspect of human life which is difficult to grasp in terms of any other domain: the momentariness of human existence.

Observe now that the example is particularly interesting in that it involves three semiotic modes: aside from the verbal and the pictorial, it also evokes the mode of sound. The latter, as is typical of this genre, is cued metonymically, with the image of a huge bell functioning as the metonymic vehicle for accessing the sound it produces (via the INSTRUMENT FOR SOUND metonymy). Importantly, the image-schematic concept of BOUNDEDNESS is manifested here in the sound mode, and it is the temporal boundedness of a physical

Example 3.13 "*Dostajemy ileś czasu na zaistnienie jak dźwięk*"—'Like sound we get a certain amount of time to exist'

Source: Kapusta (2014, 37).

sound that serves to provide an understanding of the timespan of a human life. In the verbal mode, this conception is cued by the expression *ileś czasu* 'some (limited span of) time', which refers to the temporal aspect of both the source and the target domains. Note, further, that on account of the multimodal construction of the source domain, the novel metaphor that underlies the meaning of this aphorism would qualify as waking. Also, as in the previous example, the explicit mention of the comparative adverb *jak* 'like' puts the multimodal simile into the focal attention of the addressee and thereby affects the activation level of this metaphor.

To close my discussion of this example, let me refer briefly to another creative use of the domain of SOUND, and specifically, of the MUSICAL SOUND, which comes from one of the *BBC-Reith* lectures that was delivered by conductor and pianist Daniel Barenboim in 2006. In the course of his five-lecture series titled "Life is music", Barenboim resorts to his music-derived knowledge about life with the aim of convincing his audience that music can become something that is used not to escape from the world, but rather to understand it. As I have argued elsewhere (Górska 2010, 2018c), on a number of occasions Barenboim's rhetoric involved his creative verbo-musical metaphors, with MUSIC as the source domain and LIFE as the target concept. In his first lecture, however, when he aimed to discuss the nature of a musical sound and the tragic element in music, he reversed the domains and, having observed that unless he sustains a certain amount of energy to a sound "it will die", he played a single C-sharp note on the piano and then characterized its duration by saying that "this is the duration of life of this C sharp produced by my finger on this piano".[19] For Barenboim, this example was meant to illustrate a "connection between the inexpressible content of music and in many ways the inexpressible content of life" (Lecture 1). Considering this observation in the context of our discussion of Example 3.13, we can now add that, in a way, this verbo-pictorial aphorism provides an understanding of "the inexpressible content of life".

3.4 Conclusions

In the literature on the subject (Lakoff and Turner 1989; Kövecses 2002, 2005), conventional metaphors in terms of which we conceptualize human life in our culture include: LIFE IS A JOURNEY, LIFE IS A GAME, LIFE IS A PRECIOUS POSSESSION, LIFE IS A (THEATRE) PLAY, LIFE IS A STORY, LIFE IS WAR, LIFE IS COMPROMISE, LIFE IS BONDAGE, LIFE IS A BURDEN, LIFE IS A DAY, LIFE IS LIGHT, LIFE IS A YEAR, LIFE IS FLUID IN THE BODY. Dwelling upon the range of conventional patterns they had identified, Lakoff and Turner expressed their astonishment in words that were adopted as the *motto* for this case study:

> [w]hat is remarkable [. . .] is not how many ways we have of conceiving of life, but how few. Where one might expect hundreds of ways of making sense of our most fundamental mysteries, the number of *basic* metaphorical conceptions of life turns out to be very small. Though these can be combined and elaborated in novel ways and expressed in infinite ways, that infinity is fashioned from the same small set of basic metaphors".
>
> (Lakoff and Turner 1989, 26)

Quite clearly, this conclusion also applies to the multimodal rendering of LIFE that was the topic of this chapter. We have seen that, except for two examples in section 3.3, Janusz Kapusta's verbo-pictorial aphorisms are all based on conventional metaphors, and it is their creative reworking in either one mode or the two modes in combination that accounts for their novelty.

Beyond doubt, the LIFE IS A JOURNEY metaphor was evoked as the most common pattern providing an understanding of diverse aspects of LIFE, with the PATH schema cued monomodally or across modes (section 3.1). A purely pictorial activation of PATH was evident only in Example 3.6, while in other cartoons this concept was rendered salient by minimal visual means (e.g., a road sign and a road-sign-like vehicle in Example 3.1; a section of a road in Example 3.4, or a huge suitcase in Example 3.6, each functioning as a metonymic vehicle for PATH) combined with conventional metaphoric expressions (e.g., *droga* 'path' in Example 3.2, *podróż* 'journey' in Examples 3.3, 3.4, and 3.5; or motion verbs that evoke PATH metonymically, e.g. *wynurzać się* 'emerge from' and *powracać* 'come back' in Example 3.7). It is remarkable also that in Examples 3.1 and 3.2, the target concept of LIFE was fully implicit, and yet its activation would seem unavoidable for integrating the verbal and the pictorial expression into a coherent multimodal message. This, in turn, indicates that, as a highly entrenched conceptual metaphor, LIFE IS A JOURNEY requires minimal context for its activation. Crucially, the earlier discussion makes it evident that this metaphor plays a crucial role in our understanding of LIFE across the two modes, allowing us to structure it in terms of the basic logic of the PATH schema that clusters together most prominently with the schema of SELF-PROPELLED MOTION. Deeply rooted in our preconceptual embodied experience, these schemas are directly meaningful to us, and their activation as a metaphorical source domain requires minimal verbal and/or visual context. It is notable that Forceville and Jeulink (2011), when concluding their study of animation films, observe that "SPG [the SOURCE-PATH-GOAL schema] is triggered on the basis of a film's visuals and sound alone; language is not necessary for its activation" (2011, 54).

It needs to be observed, however briefly, that the basicness of LIFE IS A JOURNEY has been confirmed in different experimental studies of verbal metaphors. In a small survey-based comparative study of metaphorical conceptualization of LIFE, Kuczok (2016) showed that, in the group of twenty Polish informants, this metaphor was the most common choice, while in the two other groups of twenty Americans and Hungarians (Kövecses 2005, 84), it ranked as the third; for the American group, the first two options were LIFE IS A PRECIOUS POSSESSION and LIFE IS A GAME,[20] while the Hungarians preferred LIFE IS A STRUGGLE and LIFE IS A COMPROMISE. We should add that, for Hungarians, this ranking of LIFE IS A JOURNEY has been confirmed in a recent large-scale survey-based study of metaphorical conceptualizations of LIFE by contemporary Hungarian teenagers, whose most common choice was the GAME metaphor (see Tables 3.2 and 3.3 in Benczes and Ságvári 2018).[21]

The prominent role of LIFE IS A JOURNEY also follows from a cross-linguistic study of English and Turkish individuals by Özçalişkan (2003), who compared Lakoff and Turner's (1989) analysis of the English data with the Turkish data collected from a variety of sources, such as literary texts, song lyrics, newspapers, news bulletins on television, and everyday spontaneous speech. Interestingly, Özçalişkan shows that, even though this metaphor is shared by the two cultures, a cross-linguistic variation emerges in its poetic uses in Turkish folk poetry, where a common extension is based on the concept of a shared journey, with a typical image of a caravan, "where a group of people 'walk their life' together heading towards death" (2003, 310). At this point, it may be observed that the verbo-pictorial aphorisms on LIFE from section 3.2 do not make any explicit reference to the conception of a shared journey, and yet, by making statements about human life in general, they also evoke an image of co-travellers who are on the same journey as we all are.

Aside from the most common multimodal reworking of LIFE IS A JOURNEY (and an implicit activation of LIFE IS LIGHT in Example 3.7), we have seen also how two other conventional metaphors—LIFE IS A GAME and LIFE IS A SHOW[22]—were creatively employed to provide a novel understanding of the target concept (section 3.3). Here again elaborations and extensions of conventional mappings as well as combining several metaphors were the main mechanisms, however, there were also two examples of the questioning of the adequacy of LIFE IS A GAME (Examples 3.8 and 3.9). And in line with CMT, the "truly" novel metaphors of LIFE in the multimodal discourse analysed in this chapter turned out to be sporadic. As expected, they served to highlight aspects of the target concept that go beyond the conventional patterns, such as the individual responsibility for the aesthetic quality of one's life and the momentariness of human existence.

The relevance of our findings for multimodal research is also notable. Corroborating the account of EMOTION concepts in Chapter 2, this study provides further support to the dynamic theory of metaphor, since it makes it apparent that the degree of overlap of the elements cued in the two modes varies considerably (from a verbal or pictorial monomodal to a bi-modal cuing) and, by the same token, activation levels of metaphoric source and target domains are gradable and dynamic. It was argued that, aside from such observable metaphoricity indicators, the novelty of the mapping should also be included among the factors that may increase the metaphor's activation level. As in Chapter 2 (see Examples 2.1 and 2.2), the analysis of aphorisms in this chapter has indicated that the overall verbo-pictorial context and the genre-specific integration of the aphorism's meaning that aims at solving a verbo-pictorial riddle and building a unified conception may bring about an abstract target concept for which there are no explicit metaphoricity indicators into the focal attention and thereby render the implicit metaphor "awake" (see Examples 3.1 and 3.2).

Finally, as in Chapter 2, in a number of cartoons considered in this chapter we have also seen that, in the multimodal meaning construction, there is a tight bond between conceptual metaphor and metonymy with the latter providing points of access for the activation of metaphoric target domains. Put in a distant perspective, this finding provides supportive evidence for the cognitive claim regarding the conceptual nature of both metaphor and metonymy.

Notes

1. This section is revised and expanded from "The PATH schema in verbo-pictorial aphorisms on LIFE", which appeared in *Route 66: From Deep Structures to Surface Meanings. A Festschrift for Henryk Kardela on his 66th Birthday*, 219–235, edited by Przemysław Łozowski, and Adam Głaz. Lublin: Maria Curie-Skłodowska University Press (2017b). It is reprinted with kind permission from Maria Curie-Skłodowska University Press, Lublin, Poland [http://wydawnictwo.umcs.eu].
2. For the theory of conceptual metonymy adopted here, see Chapter 1, note 24. Incidentally, the directional symbols also function as "visual vectors" in the sense of Bateman (2014, 59; see note 19 in Chapter 2).
3. The conceptual link between path and motion has received a lot of attention in research on "subjective/abstract" motion (Langacker 1987), also known as "fictive" motion (Talmy 1996). Specifically, motion as a well-entrenched "affordance" of paths is given as a plausible cognitive basis for this phenomenon (cf. Matsumoto 1996, 189, and the literature cited therein). Note, further, that experimental research has provided an extensive body of evidence showing that fictive motion is processed in terms of some conception of actual motion, which entails, of course, some conception of a physical path (see Matlock 2010; Richardson and Matlock 2007).
4. For experimental evidence in favour of the psychological reality of the LIFE IS A JOURNEY metaphor, see Katz and Taylor (2008).

A Multimodal Case Study of LIFE   71

5. Note that the metaphorical interpretation of the world as "heading somewhere" depends on the same two primary metaphors that underlie the JOURNEY metaphor of LIFE, namely PURPOSES ARE DESTINATIONS and ACTION IS MOTION. At the generic level, these metaphors, as constitutive parts of the so-called LOCATION EVENT-STRUCTURE METAPHOR SYSTEM, provide understanding of any kind of LONG-TERM PURPOSEFUL ACTIVITY in terms of the JOURNEY domain (Lakoff 1993; Lakoff and Johnson 1999, 178–194).

   For a study of embodied simulation in the interpretation of diverse metaphors that take the JOURNEY source domain, see Ritchie (2008); for a corpus-based research on the interaction of people's mental imagery for their embodied experience of paths and roads and the metaphoric use of *path* and *road* in English discourse on LIFE and other kinds of PURPOSEFUL ACTIVITIES, see Johansson Falck and Gibbs (2012).

6. Other culturally salient instances would include CAREER IS A JOURNEY and LOVE IS A JOURNEY. Note also that even though we can change paths *during* our journey, at a particular stage we are still following only one of them. Interestingly, Forceville (2013) provides an ingenious example of how, relying on affordances of the animation genre, Mirosław Kijowicz, a Polish animation film director, has creatively questioned this aspect of our life choices in his film *Droga* 'The Road' (1971, www.animacjapolska.pl/film,7790,,Droga--.html). As Forceville describes it, on arriving at a Y-crossing the protagonist "hesitates, wondering whether he will go left or right. He begins going left, but quickly retraces his steps to turn right, then hesitates again. Then the man splits (is split?) into two, his left half taking the left road, his right half taking the right road. The film follows his right half"; in the course of time, when the right part meet the left one, it turns out that "his left half has grown taller than his right half. Nonetheless, the two unequal halves merge into a somewhat awkward whole again, and the man pursues his way" (2013, 5). And Forceville goes on to conclude that even though he is whole again, these different past experiences "will remain with him from now on"; whether this is to be interpreted as a happy or sad ending of the film is left open (see 2013, 7).

7. For more on metaphorical highlighting and hiding, see Kövecses (2002, chap. 7).

8. Recall that the different wordings of this metaphor reflect different labels of its image schematic source, which is referred to as the BOUNDED SPACE (LOCATION) or the CONTAINER schema (see also example 2.3).

9. This verb only has the temporal sense in Polish.

10. For metaphorical conceptions of the life-cycle, see Lakoff and Turner (1989, 87–89).

11. For more on UP-DOWN, see note 28, section 1.4.

12. For more on movement (and speed) lines, also referred to as "pictorial runes" (Forceville 2011a), see Forceville, El Refaie, and Meesters (2014); Szawerna (2017, chap. 3).

13. Note that the FRONT-BACK schema is cued only visually.

14. In CMT, each source domain has its "meaning focus" (or "meaning foci") that reflects (reflect) generally shared basic knowledge about the source that "is typical of most cases of the source; and [. . .] is characteristic of the source only" (Kövecses 2002, 110). The mappings which "carry over" the main meaning focus/foci of the source onto the target domain are called "central mappings"; their differentiation also relies, among others, on their cultural characteristics—they "reflect major human concerns relative to the source in question" and linguistically, they motivate "metaphorical expressions that dominate a metaphor" (Kövecses 2002, 112). Arguably, the idea of winning and losing constitutes the

meaning focus of the GAME domain, and on this account, the mapping SUCCESS/ FAILURE IN LIFE IS WINNING/LOSING IN A GAME is one of the central mappings of LIFE IS A GAME. This mapping qualifies as central also in terms of its cultural characteristics: it reflects the well-known reason why people get involved in games. Note also that verbal metaphors that are motivated by this mapping are common and well-entrenched in languages like Polish, e.g.: (i) *postawić wszystko na jedną kartę* 'to bet everything on one card'; (ii) *wygrać los na loterii* 'win the lottery'; (iii) *gra o dużą stawkę* 'a game for high stakes'; (iv) *przegrać życie* 'to lose life'; or English (cf. the English equivalents of the Polish expressions in (i)—(iv)); for more on central mappings, see Kövecses (2002, 110–112).

15. Recall that this metaphor is experientially motivated by the BOUNDED SPACE image schema (see also Example 2.3).
16. For Polish, the novelty of LIFE IS A MOVIE is also indicated by the results of a small-scale survey-based study of metaphorical conceptualizations of LIFE by Kuczok (2016), where this metaphor was not attested.

    It is notable that Benczes and Ságvári (2018), in their large-scale survey-based study of metaphorical construals of LIFE by contemporary Hungarian teenagers, have established that LIFE IS A MOVIE ranked as the eighth (out of 32) metaphorical conceptualization of this concept (see Table 2 in Benczes and Ságvári 2018, 133). By contrast, this metaphor was not listed among the ten most frequent metaphorical conceptualizations of LIFE by Hungarian informants (of different age groups) in a small-scale survey-based study reported by Kövecses (2005, 84); Benczes and Ságvári's results (2018) can thus be said to imply that, in the group of Hungarian teenagers, the metaphor has been changing into a conventional pattern of thought. The question of whether this trend is characteristic of Polish teenagers, while interesting, remains open.
17. For GOOD IS LIGHT and BAD IS DARK, see also Chapter 1, note 25 and Example 1.2.
18. Interestingly, in the Aboriginal communities of Australia, the metaphor KNOWING IS HEARING is the dominant pattern (Evans and Wilkins 2000).
19. Lecture 1 titled "In the beginning was sound", delivered by Daniel Barenboim at Cadogan Hall, London, BBC Radio *Reith Lectures 2006*. Accessed June 10, 2006. www.bbc.co.uk/radio4/reith2006/lecture1.shtml.

    Note that this personification of sound qualifies as a verbo-musical metaphor on account of both the distribution of the metaphorical source and target across two modes and the crucial role of the verbal context (cf. *the duration of the life of this C sharp*) in interpreting the duration of the sound played by Barenboim in terms of the life-span of a human being.
20. For more on LIFE IS A GAME as a pervasive pattern in American culture, see also Ching (1993).
21. In their study, Benczes and Ságvári tested 2,594 informants, and their data sample included 890 items (2018, 131–132).
22. Interestingly, providing ample linguistic and multimodal data, Yu (2017) extensively argues that, for the Chinese, the conceptual metaphor LIFE IS AN OPERA, as a more specific instance of LIFE IS A SHOW, constitutes a highly salient cultural model of life, which frames their attitudes towards life and their worldview on life (for more on linguistic evidence for this metaphor, see also Yu and Jia 2016).

4 Conclusion

Viewed from a distant perspective, this book has shown that the static composition of cartoons as a genre makes them a valuable source of insights into how we understand abstract concepts across the verbal and the pictorial modes in multimodal discourse. Of these, the most general insight pertains to the fact that, in Janusz Kapusta's cartoons that were analysed in this book as a more specific genre of verbo-pictorial aphorisms, the image-schematic reasoning underlies, on the one hand, the static depictions of the drawings and, on the other hand, their integration with the verbal mode. Providing the skeletal structure to the multimodal discourse, image schemas guide the inferencing process that is motivated by the logic of our preconceptual bodily experiences. We have seen, again and again, that this "bodily" logic, via the source-to-target mappings, is inherent in the metaphor-based reasoning about diverse EMOTION concepts (Chapter 2) and about LIFE (Chapter 3). In effect, various creative verbo-pictorial metaphors that we arrived at in the course of the analysis of Janusz Kapusta's aphorisms turned out to be rooted in primary metaphors that form the core of our abstract thought. This finding, it needs to be emphasized, corroborates the results of multimodal research that includes diverse case studies of, among others, visual rhetoric (Ortiz 2010); gestural enactments of Paul Klee's pictures (Mittelberg 2013); user-interface design (Hurtienne 2014); a food-design event (Tseng 2017); and of the dynamic genre of film (see, e.g., Forceville 2006, 2011b, 2016a, 2017; Forceville and Jeulink 2011; Ortiz 2011, 2014; Potsch and Williams 2012; Forceville and Renckens 2013; Winter 2014; Forceville and Paling 2018).

Another type of insight pertains to the dual role of metonymy in verbo-pictorial discourse. On the one hand, we have seen that, similarly to the gestural forms of expression (see Mittelberg, and Waugh 2009, 2014), it often functions as a conceptual tool for activating the metaphoric source domain; suffice it to recall the drawing of a suitcase providing a metonymic shortcut to the source domain of JOURNEY in Examples 2.9 and 3.5 or the image of a

74 Conclusion

bell that functions as a metonymic vehicle for accessing the domain of SOUND in Example 3.13. And on the other hand, our discussion showed that metonymy is the main mechanism that serves to overcome the static composition of the cartoons as a genre (see also Górska 2018b). We saw on several occasions how from a single stage of an action depicted in the drawing—via the (REPRESENTATIVE) STAGE OF AN ACTION FOR THE ACTION metonymy—a dynamic interpretation of the drawing and of the whole verbo-pictorial aphorism arises. Other recurring metonymies that opened up mental access to various processual concepts include: PATH FOR MOTION, INSTRUMENT FOR ACTION, OBJECT INVOLVED IN THE ACTION FOR THE ACTION, and EFFECT OF EMOTION FOR EMOTION (CAUSE). It needs to be also observed that in his drawings Janusz Kapusta resorts to conventional means for expressing different aspects of temporal concepts in static visuals which are known as "movement" and "speed lines" or "pictorial runes" (see note 12 in Chapter 3) only occasionally (Example 3.7 is the only such instance in the analysed sample) and, therefore, metonymic thinking is the main tool that allows for a dynamic interpretation of the static composition of his drawings and, in effect, the basis for establishing cohesive ties with the processual concepts expressed verbally.

For discourse research, in turn, the two case studies of EMOTION concepts (Chapter 2) and of LIFE (Chapter 3) are revealing in that they demonstrate the role of genre in interpreting abstract concepts that were the theme of Janusz Kapusta's multimodal discourse—his cartoons from the Polish weekly *Plus Minus*. Classified sometimes as philosophical drawings, in this study they were analysed as a more specific genre of verbo-pictorial aphorisms. To the readers of *Plus Minus*, where they have been published almost every week since 2003, they constitute a well-established genre. In discourse research, this observation is crucial since, as Tseronis and Forceville put it: "[o]nce we understand a given instance of multimodal discourse as being attributable to a specific genre, we instantaneously, and presumably largely automatically, activate all the expectations aroused by that genre's conventions" (Tseronis and Forceville 2017a, 8, and the literature cited therein; see also Caballero 2016). Arguably, then, the regular readers of this Polish weekly recognize instantaneously Janusz Kapusta's verbo-pictorial aphorisms as a conceptual riddle that they are invited to solve. They would also expect that their solution of this kind of a riddle would have as its "intellectual reward" some novel understanding of the issue raised by the aphorism, be it some aspect of emotional life (see Chapter 2), human life (see Chapter 3), wisdom and stupidity (see Górska 2018a), or many other topics that include society, religion, politics, and the world and universe at large. Moreover, once they interpret the depicted protagonist as a visual blend of a Buddha and a chess pawn, they would know that Kapusta's verbo-pictorial aphorisms can be interpreted from two different perspectives: that of an enlightened sage (a Buddha) or

Conclusion 75

of Everyman (a pawn).[1] Let us recall that this aspect of his artworks was made evident in the cover of his book (see Figure 1.3) titled *Plus Minus* with a notable subtitle *Podręcznik do myślenia*—'A Handbook for Thinking', which explicitly invites the reader to embark on an intellectual journey. To a new audience not acquainted with his work earlier, the book title helps in "deciphering" the goals and expectation of the verbo-pictorial aphorisms as a genre as well as in understanding the author-audience relation.

Recall now that the specificity of the genre was also argued to play a key role in activating abstract target concepts for which there were no explicit cues in any of the two modes. This was the case in Example 2.1, where the target domain of EMOTIONAL DISTANCE was not activated explicitly. Referring to the genre of verbo-pictorial aphorisms which expects the addressee to interpret the verbally and pictorially conveyed message not at its face value, but as a conceptual riddle that he is invited to solve, it was claimed that, in the context of what the verbal mode specifies, the spatial proximity of the two figures in the drawing invites the activation of the emotion domain as the aphorism's main theme. Similarly, in the case of Examples 3.1 and 3.2, even though the target concept of LIFE was fully implicit, it was suggested that its activation is unavoidable for integrating the verbal and the pictorial expression into a coherent multimodal message. Examples of this kind were taken as evidence for postulating a revised model of the dynamic theory of metaphoricity (see section 1.3), which would accommodate the fact that in the genre of verbo-pictorial aphorisms, the construction of an abstract target concept that is evoked without any explicit metaphoricity indicators may bring the implicit notion into the focal attention of the addressee, and thereby "awaken" the metaphor that provides the relevant understanding. Likewise, the novelty of the mapping which is cued in one mode or across modes was included among the factors that increase the level of metaphoricity. In more general terms, this implies that in the discourse of verbo-pictorial aphorisms, the level of metaphoricity cannot be established as a simple measure of the "observable metaphoricity indicators" (see section 1.3) for two reasons: on the one hand, the overall verbo-pictorial context may render a fully implicit target concept highly salient and, on the other hand, the novelty of a mapping (whether monomodal or multimodal), on account of its attention-drawing effects, may also contribute to a higher metaphoricity level.

A reader interested in the method of analysis of multimodal discourse that was presented in section 1.4 might have noticed that, of the three versions of the proposed method, the "verbal-mode-first" procedure was employed as often as the one in which the two modes were considered together (cf., respectively, analyses of Examples 2.3; 2.4; 2.5; 2.7; 2.8; 2.10; 3.3; 3.5; 3.8; 3.9, and 2.1; 2.2; 2.6; 3.1; 3.2; 3.4; 3.6; 3.7; 3.10; 3.11; 3.12; 3.13), while the "pictorial-mode-first" procedure was used in the analysis of one aphorism only (Example 2.9). This difference reflects the specificity of the genre in which—by default—it is the verbal mode that evokes the metaphorical target concept, while the close interplay of the two modes guides the interpretation of the conceptual riddle posed by a given verbo-pictorial aphorism. It is notable also that the procedure in which the two modes were considered together was useful not only in the case of a high overlap between the verbal and pictorial modes of expression (as in Example 3.7 or 3.11), but also in cases where the implicit target concept was rendered salient by the interplay of the two modes (Examples 2.1; 3.1; 3.2). Crucially, in all three variants of the method the aim was to establish cross-modal cohesive ties in a motivated manner, i.e., in terms of image schemas and their inferential structure. As was already noted, the main advantage of the proposed analytical procedure is that it stands a good chance of including in its scope aspects of multimodal construction which might be easily omitted in other approaches. This advantage of the proposed method comes to the fore when we take a broader perspective of research in multimodal argumentation and rhetoric; as Tseronis and Forceville observe when concluding their overview of such research, "most studies so far tend to consider the various modes that interact in a given multimodal text independently of each other, and thereby overlook the functions and effects that arise from a combination thereof" (Tseronis and Forceville 2017a, 15–16). This cognitive linguistic study, by contrast, relying on image-schematic structuring of the verbal and the pictorial modes, focused on how the two modes interplay in providing a metaphorical understanding of abstract concepts. The dynamic theory of metaphor (Müller 2008a; Kolter et al. 2012; see section 1.3) turned out to be an adequate framework for establishing different levels of metaphoricity, with the higher activation levels reflecting a multimodal construction of the aphorisms' meaning. In its revised version proposed here, the dynamic model also accommodates the earlier discussed genre-specific interplay of the two modes and the novelty of mappings as factors that, on account of their attention-grabbing effects, may increase the metaphoricity level of a multimodal discourse.

Attention-grabbing effects are, no doubt, a relevant aspect of rhetoric, irrespective of whether it is purely verbal or multimodal. It is also generally recognized that both in verbal and in multimodal discourse, metaphor is a means of persuasion that is used to shape, reinforce, or change the response of an audience. Moreover, as Hidalgo-Downing and Kraljevic-Mujic put it: "a metaphor is potentially persuasive if it makes use of already known beliefs, shared knowledge, needs and desires in the audience. This is known as the 'anchor', or point of departure for the persuasive effect, since it originates in already accepted beliefs" (2016, 326; and the literature cited therein). It is notable that, when we consider the findings of cognitive poetics, this aspect of metaphor use can be discussed in terms of the mechanisms of reworking of the conventional conceptual metaphors "we live by", which can thus be seen as "anchoring" the conventional understanding of shared knowledge, accepted beliefs, and evaluative judgments. Importantly, this study has demonstrated that the creative multimodal discourse of Janusz Kapusta's aphorisms relies on a wide range of conventional metaphors and metonymies and, as in the case of the poetic use of language, it is through the various mechanisms of reworking of the conventional patterns that a novel understanding of the issues raised in this verbo-pictorial discourse the reader is invited to entertain. Of these mechanisms, elaboration and extension of conventional metaphorical mappings, combination of a number of conventional metaphors, as well as elaborations of conventional metonymies were the most common tools of reworking of the highly schematic conventional patterns, while the mechanism of questioning the validity of the conventional patterns of thought was used only occasionally (cf. Examples 2.4; 3.8 and 3.9). And, unsurprisingly, truly novel metaphors were a rarity—in the analysed sample we encounter two such instances in section 3.3, where LIFE was understood in terms of the source domain of PAINTING (Example 3.12) and of SOUND (Example 3.13).

The verbo-pictorially reworked conventional patterns, just like the novel verbo-pictorial metaphors in terms of which Janusz Kapusta's aphorisms are expressed, characteristically for multimodal discourse in general, give rise to highly iconic and condensed meanings. The high iconicity arises from the interplay of two factors—the multimodal construction, on the one hand, and the high iconicity of the pictorial semiotic mode, on the other hand. In particular, through multimodal construction particular aspects of the aphorisms' meaning are as if "pointed out" more than once, and thereby—in terms of the iconic principle of quantity—have more content and are rendered more salient (see, e.g., the verbo-pictorial cueing of EMOTIONS ARE FORCES and EMOTIONS ARE BONDS in Example 2.2 or of the source domain of SOUND in Example 3.13). As I argued elsewhere (Górska 2014a, 30–32), this function of multimodal metaphors becomes particularly interesting when put in the perspective of how spoken and signed languages represent spatial structure. The latter issue was extensively discussed by Talmy (2003), who provides ample evidence supporting the claim that, unlike in spoken languages, in signed languages spatial representations are largely iconic, showing far greater "fidelity to the characteristics of visual perception" (Talmy 2003, 235). Note that in this context iconicity refers to a correspondence of degree or kind between a representation and what it represents (Talmy 2003, 242). This kind of iconicity is, according to Talmy, evident in the coding of aspects of a motion event by the so-called signed classifier system, which is to a large extent iconic with the parsing of the corresponding motion event in visual perception. Another difference pertains to discreteness vs. gradience as a basic organizing principle: in the verbal mode of expression, the norms are discrete spatial elements

78 Conclusion

(typically coded by distinct morphemes), while in the signed languages the norms are spatial categories (of the classifier system) which are gradient in nature. And so in this case, again, signed languages, unlike the verbal mode, exhibit a high degree of iconic coding of meaning. Seen in this light, co-verbal multimodal metaphors, and those which have spatial image schemas as their source domain in particular are means of increasing iconicity of the verbal code (see also Górska 2014a, 31).

The verbo-pictorial discourse that was analysed in this study provides further support to this claim. We have seen again and again that, thanks to the characteristic affordances of the pictorial mode, several aspects of meaning were evoked in "one shot"—in a highly iconic image of a single drawing; recall, e.g.: the spatial/emotional closeness/distance of the two figures in Example 2.1; the pictorial cueing of the LINK and the BOUNDED SPACE image schemas in Example 2.3 that motivates the construal of human relationships as BONDS and ENCLOSURES at the same time; a number of emotions "enacted" by the protagonist in Example 2.9(b); the pictorial rendition of the traveller as 'the changing landscape' in Example 3.4; or a fountain-like beam of light which increases in size and changes in colour from dark to white, gradually encircling the protagonist and, with respect to him, heading from the back towards the front in Example 3.7. Note, additionally, that this kind of iconic coding that characterizes schematic drawings of Kapusta's aphorisms is even more evident in "the iconic representation of pictures", which, as Kjeldsen argues, "offers a visual presence, immediacy and realism that cannot be matched by words" (Kjeldsen 2015b, 213). Moreover, this characteristic of the pictorial mode is highly relevant when we consider what Kjeldsen calls "symbolic condensation", i.e., "the condensing of different sensations, words, and ideas into one pictorial or multimodal representation" (2016a, 265). On his account, symbolic condensation "can be both emotional (evoking emotions) and rational (evoking arguments and reasoning)" (Kjeldsen 2018, 86). Crucially, "the rhetorical and argumentative value of symbolic condensation is that it allows for a cueing and the evoking of thoughts and feelings" (Kjeldsen 2018, 86).

Note now that the symbolic condensation of these two kinds is also evident in the multimodal discourse that was analysed in this book. Seen in terms of the cognitive linguistic theory, symbolic condensation resides in evoking, via multimodal or monomodal cues, metaphorical and metonymic patterns of reasoning—both conventional and creatively reworked—in a given verbo-pictorial aphorism. Importantly, forming two intertwined aspects of numerous verbo-pictorial aphorisms, the emotional condensation was commonly achieved through a pictorial cueing of image-schematic source domains and activating primary metaphors in terms of which we grasp the emotive and subjective aspects of our experience. One of these was the UP-DOWN schema

Conclusion 79

and the primary metaphors POSITIVE IS UP and NEGATIVE IS DOWN which are based on it.² Recall, for instance, the verbo-pictorially construed HAPPINESS and UNHAPPINESS in Example 2.8; or the image of the protagonist as a simultaneous winner and loser in Example 3.9. In Example 3.6, on the other hand, the cueing of positive and negative emotions in terms of UP-DOWN was combined with the construal of SIGNIFICANCE/IMPORTANCE in terms of the BIG-SMALL schema, and the inferential structure of these two schemas triggered the evaluation of the depicted initial state of 'being up and big' (hence active, important, and in the peak of power) as positive, and the final state of 'the reduced body being down—almost completely submerged in the ground' (hence, unable to act, unimportant, and powerless)—as negative. Recall also the memorable construal of REAL WORRIES in Example 2.9(b), where the size of the suitcase, which has been given focal prominence in the drawing, was regarded as a pictorial cue for conceiving the intensity of the emotion in terms of the BIG-SMALL schema.

Needless to say, one would value highly putting the results of the analyses presented in this book to an empirical test. The experimental line of research on visual and multimodal discourse, though recognized as a welcome trend in multimodality (see Kjeldsen 2016b, 2018; Tseronis and Forceville 2017a), is still at an early stage (for overviews see Bateman 2014; Bateman, Wildfeuer, Hiippala 2017). In cognitive linguistic research, the notable exceptions include Pérez-Sobrino's (2017) investigation of advertisements; Abdel-Raheem's (2018) study of op-eds; and, to my knowledge, the first experimental study of artworks and satirical cartoons by Dąbrowska (2019). I believe, however, that the image-schema-based method of analysis of multimodal discourse that was developed in this book allows for formulating several testable hypotheses: on how the modes involved interact in conveying a unified conception; on the role of conventional patterns of thought (image schemas, conceptual metaphors, and metonymies) in creative multimodal discourse; on the level of metaphoricity of a given multimodal communicative act and factors that have attention-grabbing effects; and on how a given multimodal discourse is understood and received. I should add also that, since in this book my analyses aimed at a broad interpretation of Janusz Kapusta's aphorisms which would accommodate both explicit and implicit aspects of meaning, designing an experiment which would establish whether my renditions of the aphorisms' verbo-pictorial message are shared by the public will not be an easy task. In particular, there will be no easy way to find whether the subjects were willing to pay due attention to the task or just took a cursory look at the screen, which would, in effect, be highly likely to skew the results. Keeping this qualification in mind, an audience-response study (with the use of, e.g., questionnaire methods) may be expected to establish a range of the target audience's interpretations, which could then be compared with the analyses proposed in this book. Going beyond the scope of this book, the latter objective, just like testing the earlier mentioned hypotheses, however intriguing and valuable, all deserve a separate empirical study of their own.

Notes

1. In this book I do not go into any analysis of visual or verbo-visual blends in terms of the blending theory (Fauconnier and Turner 1998, 2002) since, in this study, I do not intend to discuss online meaning construction (see, e.g., Górska 2010, 2018c), but aim at analysing the specific genre of verbo-pictorial discourse in terms of the conventional patterns of thought—image schemas as well as conceptual metaphors and metonymies, focusing on their role in creative understanding of abstract concepts across the two modes.
2. For an experimental study of the association between affect and UP-DOWN orientation, see Meier and Robinson (2004).

References

Abdel-Raheem, Ahmed. 2014. "The JOURNEY metaphor and moral political cognition". *Pragmatics and Cognition* 22 (3): 373–401.
Abdel-Raheem, Ahmed. 2018. *Pictorial Framing in Moral Politics*. London: Routledge.
Arnheim, Rudolf. 1969. *Visual Thinking*. Berkeley: University of California Press.
Athanasiadou, Angeliki, and Elżbieta Tabakowska, eds. 1998. *Speaking of Emotions: Conceptualisation and Expression*. Berlin: Mouton de Gruyter.
Barsalou, Lawrence W. 2008. "Grounded cognition". *Annual Review of Psychology* 59: 617–645.
Bateman, John A. 2014. *Text and Image. A Critical Introduction to the Visual/Verbal Divide*. London: Routledge.
Bateman, John, Janina Wildfeuer, and Tuomo Hiippala. 2017. *Multimodality: Foundations, Research and Analysis. A Problem-Oriented Introduction*. Berlin: De Gruyter Mouton.
Benczes, Réka, and Bence Ságvári. 2018. "Where metaphors *really* come from: Social factors as contextual influence in Hungarian teenagers' metaphorical conceptualizations of life". *Cognitive Linguistics* 29 (1): 121–154.
Brône, Geert, and Kurt Feyaerts 2004. "Assessing the SSTH and GTVH: A view from cognitive linguistics". *Humor* 17 (4): 361–372.
Caballero, Rosario. 2016. "Genre and metaphor. Use and variation across usage events". In *The Routledge Handbook of Metaphor and Language*, edited by Elena Semino, and Zsófia Demjén, 193–205. London: Routledge.
Calbris, Geneviève. 2008. "From left to right. . . : Coverbal gestures and their symbolic use of space". In *Metaphor and Gesture*, edited by Alan Cienki, and Cornelia Müller, 27–54. Amsterdam: John Benjamins.
Ching, Marvin K. L. 1993. "Games and play: Pervasive metaphors in American life". *Metaphor and Symbolic Activity* 8 (1): 43–65.
Chilton, Paul. 2009. "*Get* and the grasp schema. A new approach to conceptual modelling in image schema semantics". In *New Directions in Cognitive Linguistics*, edited by Vyvyan Evans, and Stéphanie Pourcel, 331–370. Amsterdam: John Benjamins.
Cienki, Alan. 1997. "Some properties and groupings of image schemas". In *Lexical and Syntactic Constructions and the Construction of Meaning*, edited by Marjolijn Verspoor, Ken Dong Lee, and Eve Sweetser, 3–15. Amsterdam: John Benjamins.

References

Cienki, Alan. 1998a. "Metaphoric gestures and some of their relations to verbal metaphoric expressions". In *Discourse and Cognition*, edited by Jean-Pierre Koenig, 189–204. Stanford: CSLI.

Cienki, Alan. 1998b. "Straight: An image schema and its metaphorical extensions". *Cognitive Linguistics* 9 (2): 107–149.

Cienki, Alan. 2005. "Image schemas and gesture." In *From Perception to Meaning: Image Schemas in Cognitive Linguistics*, edited by Beate Hampe, 421–442. Berlin: Mouton de Gruyter.

Cienki, Alan. 2013. "Image schemas and mimetic schemas in cognitive linguistics and gesture studies". *Review of Cognitive Linguistics* 11 (2): 417–432.

Cienki, Alan, and Cornelia Müller. 2008a. "Metaphor, gesture, and thought". In *The Cambridge Handbook of Metaphor and Thought*, edited by Raymond W. Gibbs, 483–501. Cambridge: Cambridge University Press.

Cienki, Alan, and Cornelia Müller, eds. 2008b. *Metaphor and Gesture*. Amsterdam: John Benjamins.

Cohn, Neil. 2013. *The Visual Language of Comics: Introduction to the Structure and Cognition of Sequential Images*. London: Bloomsbury.

Dąbrowska, Dorota. 2019. "Metaphor and metonymy in multimodal discourse. Case studies of selected artworks by Magdalena Abakanowicz and satirical cartoons by Paweł Kuczyński". PhD diss., University of Warsaw.

Damasio, Antonio. 2000. *The Feeling of what Happens. Body, Emotion and the Making of Consciousness*. New York: Harvester.

Dancygier, Barbara, and Eve Sweetser. 2014. *Figurative Language*. Cambridge: Cambridge University Press.

Evans, Nicholas, and David Wilkins. 2000. "In the mind's ear: The semantic extensions in the domain of perception verbs in Australian languages". *Language* 76 (3): 546–590.

Evans, Vyvyan, and Melanie Green. 2006. *Cognitive Linguistics: An Introduction*. Edinburgh: Edinburgh University Press.

Fabiszak, Małgorzata, and Anna Hebda. 2010. "Cognitive historical approaches to emotions: Pride". In *Historical Cognitive Linguistics*, edited by Margaret E. Winters, Heli Tissari, and Kathryn Allan, 261–297. Berlin: Mouton De Gruyter.

Fauconnier, Gilles, and Mark Turner. 1998. "Conceptual integration networks". *Cognitive Science* 22: 133–187.

Fauconnier, Gilles, and Mark Turner. 2002. *The Way We Think. Conceptual Blending and the Mind's Hidden Complexities*. New York: Basic Books.

Foolen, Ad. 2012. "The relevance of emotion for language and linguistics". In *Moving Ourselves, Moving others. Motion and Emotion in Intersubjectivity, Consciousness and Language*, edited by Ad Foolen, Ulrike M. Lüdke, Timothy P. Racine, and Jordan Zlatev, 349–368. Amsterdam: John Benjamins.

Foolen, Ad, Ulrike M. Lüdke, Timothy P. Racine, and Jordan Zlatev, eds. 2012. *Moving Ourselves, Moving Others. Motion and Emotion in Intersubjectivity, Consciousness and Language*. Amsterdam: John Benjamins.

Forceville, Charles. 1996. *Pictorial Metaphor in Advertising*. London: Routledge.

Forceville, Charles. 2006. "The source-path-goal schema in the autobiographical journey documentary: McElwee, Van der Keuken, Cole". *The New Review of Film and Television Studies* 4 (3): 241–261.

References

Forceville, Charles. 2011a. "Pictorial runes in *Tintin and the Picaros*". *Journal of Pragmatics* 43 (3): 875–890.

Forceville, Charles. 2011b. "The JOURNEY metaphor and the Source-Path-Goal schema in Agnès Varda's Gleaning autobiographical documentaries". In *Beyond Cognitive Metaphor Theory. Perspectives on Literary Metaphor*, edited by Monika Fludernik, 281–297. London: Routledge.

Forceville, Charles. 2013. A Course in Pictorial and Multimodal Metaphor. Lecture 7: "Structural pictorial and multimodal metaphor". Accessed October 8, 2013. projects.chass.utoronto.ca/smiotics/cyber/cforceville7.pdf

Forceville, Charles. 2016a. "The force and balance schemas in journey metaphor animations". In *Multimodality and Performance*, edited by Carla Fernandes, 8–22. Newcastle upon Tyne: Cambridge Scholars Publishing.

Forceville, Charles. 2016b. "Pictorial and multimodal metaphor." In *Handbuch Sprache im multimodalen Kontext*. [The Language in Multimodal Contexts Handbook], edited by Nina-Maria Klug, and Hartmut Stöckl, 242–261. Berlin: Mouton de Gruyter.

Forceville, Charles. 2017. "From image schema to metaphor in discourse: The force schemas in animation films". In *Metaphor, Embodied Cognition, and Discourse*, edited by Beate Hampe, 2017b, 239–256. Cambridge: Cambridge University Press.

Forceville, Charles, and Eduardo Urios-Aparisi. 2009a. "Introduction". In *Multimodal Metaphor*, edited by Charles Forceville, and Eduardo Urios-Aparisi, 3–17. Berlin: Mouton de Gruyter.

Forceville, Charles, and Eduardo Urios-Aparisi, eds. 2009b. *Multimodal Metaphor*. Berlin: Mouton de Gruyter.

Forceville, Charles, Lisa El Refaie, and Gert Meesters. 2014. "Stylistics and comics". In *Routledge Handbook of Stylistics*, edited by Michael Burke, 485–499. London: Routledge.

Forceville, Charles, and Marloes Jeulink. 2011. "The flesh and blood of embodied understanding: The Source-Path-Goal schema in animation film." *Pragmatics and Cognition* 19 (1): 37–59.

Forceville, Charles, and Sissy Paling. 2018. "The metaphorical representation of DEPRESSION in short, wordless animation films". *Visual Communication*, published ahead of print September 21, 2018, at https://doi.org/10.1177/1470357218797994

Forceville, Charles, and Thijs Renckens. 2013. "The GOOD IS LIGHT and BAD IS DARKNESS metaphors in feature films." *Metaphor and the Social World* 3 (2): 160–179.

Forceville, Charles, Tony Veale, and Kurt Feyaerts. 2010. "Balloonics: The visuals of balloons in comics". In *The Rise and reason of Comics and Graphic Literature: Critical Essays on the Form*, edited by Joyce Goggin, and Dan Hassler-Forest, 56–73. Jefferson, NC: McFarland.

Gibbs, Raymond W. 2015a. "Does deliberate metaphor theory have a future?" *Journal of Pragmatics* 90:73–76.

Gibbs, Raymond W. 2015b. "Do pragmatic signals affect conventional metaphor understanding? A failed test of deliberate metaphor theory". *Journal of Pragmatics* 90: 77–87.

Gibbs, Raymond W., and Herbert L. Colston 1995. "The cognitive psychological reality of image schemas and their transformations". *Cognitive Linguistics* 6 (4): 247–378.

References

Gibbs, Raymond W., Paula Lenz Costa Lima, and Edson Francozo 2004. "Metaphor is grounded in embodied experience". *Journal of Pragmatics* 36 (7): 1189–1210.

Górska, Elżbieta. 2010. "LIFE IS MUSIC: A case study of a novel metaphor and its use in discourse". *English Text Construction* 3 (2): 275–293. Reprinted in *Textual Choices and Discourse. A View from Cognitive Linguistics*, edited by Barbara Dancygier, José Sanders, and Lieven Vandelanotte, 2012, 137–155. Amsterdam: John Benjamins.

Górska, Elżbieta. 2014a. "Why are multimodal metaphors interesting? The perspective of verbo-visual and verbo-musical modalities". In *From Conceptual Metaphor Theory to Cognitive Ethnolinguistics. Patterns of Imagery in Language*, edited by Marek Kuźniak, Agnieszka Libura, and Michał Szawerna, 17–36. Frankfurt am Main: Peter Lang.

Górska, Elżbieta. 2014b. "The UP/DOWN orientation in language and music". In *The Body in Language. Comparative Studies of Linguistic Embodiment*, edited by Matthias Brenzinger, and Iwona Kraska-Szlenk, 177–195. Leiden: Brill.

Górska, Elżbieta. 2017a. "Text-image relations in cartoons. A case study of image schematic metaphors". *Studia Linguistica Universitatis Iagellonicae Cracoviensis* 134 (3): 219–228. doi: 10.4467/20834624SL.17.015.7089.

Górska, Elżbieta. 2017b. "The PATH schema in verbo-pictorial aphorisms on LIFE". In *Route 66: From Deep Structures to Surface Meanings. A Festschrift for Henryk Kardela on his 66th Birthday*, edited by Przemysław Łozowski, and Adam Głaz, 219–235. Lublin: Maria Curie-Skłodowska University Press.

Górska, Elżbieta. 2018a. "A multimodal portrait of WISDOM and STUPIDITY. A case study of image-schematic metaphors in cartoons". In *New Insights into the Language and Cognition interface*, edited by Rafał Augustyn, and Agnieszka Mierzwińska-Hajnos, 98–117. Newcastle upon Tyne: Cambridge Scholars Publishing.

Górska, Elżbieta. 2018b. "On metonymy in cartoons. A case study of verbo-pictorial aphorisms". A paper delivered at the *Conference of the Polish Cognitive Linguistics Association*, September 24–26, 2018, Adam Mickiewicz University, Poznań, Poland.

Górska, Elżbieta. 2018c. "From music to language and back". *Language, Mind, Culture, Society (LaMiCuS)* 2: 82–100.

Górska, Elżbieta. 2019 (in press). "Spatialization of abstract concepts in cartoons. A case study of verbo-pictorial image-schematic metaphors". In *Current Approaches to Metaphor Analysis in Discourse*, edited by Ignasi Navarro i Ferrando. Berlin: De Gruyter Mouton.

Grady, Joseph E. 1997. *Foundations of Meaning: Primary Metaphors and Primary Scenes*. Unpublished PhD diss., University of California, Berkeley.

Grady, Joseph E. 2005. "Primary metaphors as inputs to conceptual integration". *Journal of Pragmatics* 37: 1595–1614.

Grady, Joseph E., and Christopher Johnson. 2002. "Converging evidence for the notions of subscene and primary scene". In *Metaphor and Metonymy in Comparison and Contrast*, edited by René Dirven, and Ralf Pörings, 533–554. Berlin: Mouton de Gruyter.

Hampe, Beate. 2005a. "Image schemas in cognitive linguistics: Introduction". In *From Perception to Meaning. Image Schemas in Cognitive Linguistics*, edited by Beate Hampe, 2005b, 1–12. Berlin: Mouton de Gruyter.

References

Hampe, Beate, ed. 2005b. *From Perception to Meaning. Image Schemas in Cognitive Linguistics*. Berlin: Mouton de Gruyter.

Hampe, Beate. 2005c. "When *down* is not bad and *up* is not good enough: A usage-based assessment of the plus-minus parameter in image-schema theory". *Cognitive Linguistics* 16 (1): 81–112.

Hampe, Beate. 2017a. "Embodiment and discourse: Dimensions and dynamics of contemporary metaphor theory". In *Metaphor, Embodied Cognition, and Discourse*, edited by Beate Hampe, 2017b, 3–23. Cambridge: Cambridge University Press.

Hampe, Beate, ed. 2017b. *Metaphor, Embodied Cognition, and Discourse*. Cambridge: Cambridge University Press.

Heine, Bernd. 1997. *Cognitive Foundations of Grammar*. Oxford: Oxford University Press.

Hidalgo-Downing, Laura, and Blanca Kraljevic-Mujic. 2016. "Metaphor and persuasion in commercial advertising". In *The Routledge Handbook of Metaphor and Language*, edited by Elena Semino, and Zsófia Demjén, 323–336. London: Routledge.

Hurtienne, Jörn. 2014. "Non-linguistic applications of cognitive linguistics: On the usefulness of image-schematic metaphors in user interface design". In *The Bloomsbury Companion to Cognitive Linguistics*, edited by Jeannette Littlemore, and John R. Taylor, 301–324. London: Bloomsbury.

Johansson Falck, Marlene, and Raymond W. Gibbs. 2012. "Embodied motivations for metaphorical meanings". *Cognitive Linguistics* 23 (2): 251–272.

Johnson, Christopher. 1999. "Metaphor vs. conflation in the acquisition of polysemy: The case of *see*". In *Cultural, Psychological and Typological Issues in Cognitive Linguistics*, edited by Masako K. Hiraga, Chris Sinha, and Sherman Wilcox, 155–170. Amsterdam: John Benjamins.

Johnson, Mark. 1987. *The Body in the Mind: The Bodily Basis of Imagination, Reason, and Meaning*. Chicago: University of Chicago Press.

Johnson, Mark. 2005. "The philosophical significance of image schemas". In *From Perception to Meaning. Image Schemas in Cognitive Linguistics*, edited by Beate Hampe, 2005b, 15–33. Berlin and New York: Mouton de Gruyter.

Johnson, Mark. 2007. *The Meaning of the Body. Aesthetics of Human Understanding*. Chicago: University of Chicago Press.

Johnson, Mark L., and Steve Larson. 2003. "'Something in the way she moves'—metaphors of musical motion". *Metaphor and Symbol* 18 (2): 63–84.

Katz, Albert N., and Tamsen E. Taylor. 2008. "The journeys of life: Examining a conceptual metaphor with semantic and episodic memory recall". *Metaphor and Symbol* 23: 148–173.

Kimmel, Michael. 2005. "Culture regained: Situated and compound image schemas". In *From Perception to Meaning. Image Schemas in Cognitive Linguistics*, edited by Beate Hampe, 2005b, 285–310. Berlin: Mouton de Gruyter.

Kjeldsen, Jens E. 2015a. "The study of visual and multimodal argumentation". *Argumentation* 29: 115–132.

Kjeldsen, Jens E. 2015b. "The rhetoric of thick representation: How pictures render the importance and strength of an argument salient". *Argumentation* 29:197–215.

References

Kjeldsen, Jens E. 2016a. "Symbolic condensation and thick representation in visual and multimodal communication. " *Argumentation and Advocacy* 52 (4): 265–280.

Kjeldsen, Jens E. 2016b. "Studying rhetorical audiences: A call for qualitative reception studies in argumentation and rhetoric". *Informal Logic* 36: 136–158. doi: 0.22329/11^3612.4672.

Kjeldsen, Jens E. 2018. "Visual rhetorical argumentation". *Semiotica* 220: 69–94.

Kolter, Astrid, Silva H. Ladewig, Michela Summa, Cornelia Müller, Sabine C. Koch, and Thomas Fuchs. 2012. "Body memory and the emergence of metaphor in movement and speech. An interdisciplinary case study". In *Body Memory, Metaphor and Movement*, edited by Sabine C. Koch, Thomas Fuchs, Michela Summa, and Cornelia Müller, 201–226. Amsterdam: John Benjamins.

Kövecses, Zoltán. 2000. *Metaphor and Emotion: Language, Culture and Body in Human Feeling*. Cambridge: Cambridge University Press.

Kövecses, Zoltán. 2002. *Metaphor. A Practical Introduction*. Oxford: Oxford University Press.

Kövecses, Zoltán. 2005. *Metaphor in Culture. Universality and Variation*. Cambridge: Cambridge University Press.

Kövecses, Zoltán. 2008a. "Conceptual metaphor theory. Some criticisms and alternative proposals". *Annual Review of Cognitive Linguistics* 6 (1): 168–184.

Kövecses, Zoltán. 2008b. "Metaphor and emotion". In *The Cambridge Handbook of Metaphor and Thought*, edited by Raymond W. Gibbs, 2008, 380–396. Cambridge: Cambridge University Press.

Kövecses, Zoltán. 2014. "Conceptualizing emotions. A revised cognitive linguistic perspective". *Poznań Studies in Contemporary Linguistics* 50 (1): 15–28.

Kövecses, Zoltán. 2015a. *Where Metaphors Come From. Reconsidering Context in Metaphor*. New York and Oxford: Oxford University Press.

Kövecses, Zoltán. 2015b. "Surprise as a conceptual category". *Review of Cognitive Linguistics* 13 (2): 270–290.

Kövecses, Zoltán, and Günter Radden. 1998. "Metonymy: Developing a cognitive linguistic view". *Cognitive Linguistics* 9 (1): 37–77.

Kuczok, Marcin. 2016. "Precious possession, war or journey? Conceptual metaphors for life in American English, Hungarian and Polish ". In *Various dimensions of contrastive studies*, edited by Bożena Cetnarowska, Marcin Kuczok, and Marcin Zabawa, 157–170. Katowice: Wydawnictwo Uniwersytetu Śląskiego.

Ladewig, Silva H. 2014. "Creating multimodal utterances: The linear integration of gestures into speech ". In *Body—Language—Communication: An International Handbook on Multimodality in Human Interaction*, vol. 2, edited by Cornelia Müller, Alan Cienki, Ellen Fricke, Silva H. Ladewig, David McNeill, and Jana Bressem, 1662–1667. Berlin: De Gruyter Mouton.

Lakoff, George. 1987. *Women, Fire and Dangerous Things: What Categories Reveal about the Mind*. Chicago: University of Chicago Press.

Lakoff, George 1990. "The Invariance Hypothesis: Is abstract reason based on imageschemas ". *Cognitive Linguistics* 1 (1), 39–74.

Lakoff, George 1993. "The contemporary theory of metaphor ". In *Metaphor and Thought*. Second edition, edited by Andrew Ortony, 202–251. Cambridge: Cambridge University Press.

Lakoff, George, and Mark Johnson. 1980. *Metaphors We Live By*. Chicago: University of Chicago Press.
Lakoff, George, and Mark Johnson. 1999. *Philosophy in The Flesh: The Embodied Mind and its Challenge to Western Thought*. New York: Basic Books.
Lakoff, George, and Mark Turner. 1989. *More than Cool Reason. A Field Guide to Poetic Metaphor*. Chicago: University of Chicago Press.
Langacker, Ronald W. 1987. *Foundations of Cognitive Grammar*. vol. 1. *Theoretical Prerequisites*. Stanford: Stanford University Press.
Langacker, Ronald W. 1993. "Reference-point constructions". *Cognitive Linguistics* 4 (1): 1–38.
Langacker, Ronald W. 2008. *Cognitive Grammar. A Basic Introduction*. Oxford: Oxford University Press.
Littlemore, Jeannette. 2015. *Metonymy: Hidden Shortcuts in Language, Thought and Communication*. Cambridge: Cambridge University Press.
Macagno, Fabrizio, and Benedetta Zavatta. 2014. "Reconstructing metaphorical meaning". *Argumentation* 28 (4): 453–488. doi: 10.1007/s10503–014–9329-z.
Macaranas, Anna, Alissa N. Antle, and Bernhard E. Riecke. 2012. "Bridging the gap: Attribute and spatial metaphors for tangible interface design". In *Proceedings of the 6th International Conference on Tangible and Embedded Interaction* 2012, 161–168. New York: ACM Press.
Mandler, Jean, and Cristóbal Págan Cánovas. 2014. "On defining image schemas". *Language and Cognition* 6 (4): 510–532.
Matlock, Teenie. 2010. "Abstract motion is no longer abstract". *Language and Cognition* 2 (2): 243–260.
Matsumoto, Yo. 1996. "Subjective motion and English and Japanese verbs". *Cognitive Linguistics* 7 (2): 183–226.
Matthews, Justin L., and Teenie Matlock. 2011. "Understanding the link between spatial distance and social distance". *Social Psychology* 42 (3): 185–192.
Meier, Brian P., and Michael D. Robinson. 2004. "Why the sunny side is up: Association between affect and vertical position". *Psychological Science* 15 (4): 243–247.
Mittelberg, Irene. 2010. "Geometric and image-schematic patterns in gesture space". In *Language, Cognition, and Space*, edited by Vyvyan Evans, and Paul Chilton, 351–385. London: Equinox.
Mittelberg, Irene. 2013. "Balancing acts: Image schemas and force dynamics as experiential essence in pictures by Paul Klee and their gestural enactments". In *Language and the Creative Mind*, edited by Mike Borkent, Barbara Dancygier, and Jennifer Hinnell, 325–346. Stanford: CSLI.
Mittelberg, Irene, and Gina Joue. 2017. "Source actions ground metaphor via metonymy: Toward a frame-based account of gestural action in multimodal discourse". In *Metaphor, Embodied Cognition and Discourse*, edited by Beate Hampe, 2017b, 119–137. Cambridge: Cambridge University Press.
Mittelberg, Irene, and Linda R. Waugh. 2009. "Metonymy first, metaphor second: A cognitive-semiotic approach to multimodal figures of thought in co-speech gesture". In *Multimodal Metaphor*, edited by Charles Forceville, and Eduardo Urios-Aparisi, 2009b, 329–356. Berlin: Mouton de Gruyter.

References

Mittelberg, Irene, and Linda R. Waugh. 2014. "Gestures and metonymy". In *Body—Language—Communication. An International Handbook on Multimodality in Human Interaction*, vol. 2, edited by Cornelia Müller, Alan Cienki, Ellen Fricke, Silva H. Ladewig, David McNeill, and Jana Bressem, 1747–1766. Berlin: De Gruyter Mouton.

Müller, Cornelia. 2008a. *Metaphors Dead and Alive, Sleeping and Waking. A Dynamic View*. Chicago: Chicago University Press.

Müller, Cornelia. 2008b. "What gestures reveal about the nature of metaphor". In *Metaphor and Thought*, edited by Alan Cienki, and Cornelia Müller, 219–245. Amsterdam: John Benjamins.

Müller, Cornelia. 2017. "Waking metaphors: Embodied cognition in multimodal discourse". In *Metaphor, Embodied Cognition, and Discourse*, edited by Beate Hampe, 2017b, 297–316. Cambridge: Cambridge University Press.

Müller, Cornelia, and Alan Cienki. 2009. "Words, gestures, and beyond: Forms of multimodal metaphor in the use of spoken language". In *Multimodal Metaphor*, edited by Charles Forceville, and Eduardo Urios-Aparisi, 2009b, 297–328. Berlin: Mouton de Gruyter.

Müller, Cornelia, Silva H. Ladewig, and Jana Bressem. 2013. "Gestures and speech from a linguistic perspective: A new field and its history". In *Body—Language—Communication. An International Handbook on Multimodality in Human Interaction*, vol. 2, edited by Cornelia Müller, Alan Cienki, Ellen Fricke, Silva H. Ladewig, David McNeill, and Jana Bressem, 55–81. Berlin: De Gruyter Mouton.

Müller, Cornelia, and Susanne Tag. 2010. "The dynamics of metaphor: Foregrounding and activating metaphoricity in conversational interaction". *Cognitive Semiotics* 6: 85–120.

Newman, John. 2017. "EAT, DRINK, MAN, WOMAN, and all that: The linguistics of ordinary human experience". A plenary lecture given at *International Cognitive Linguistics Conference* 14, July 1–14, 2017, Tartu, Estonia.

Ortiz, María J. 2010. "Visual rhetoric: Primary metaphors and symmetric object alignment". *Metaphor and Symbol* 25 (3): 162–180.

Ortiz, María J. 2011. "Primary metaphors and monomodal visual metaphors". *Journal of Pragmatics* 43 (6): 1568–1580.

Ortiz, María J. 2014. "Visual manifestations of primary metaphors through *mise-en-scène* techniques". *Image and Narrative* 15 (1): 5–16.

Özçalişkan, Şeyda. 2003. "*In a caravanserai with two doors I am walking day and night*: Metaphors of death and life in Turkish". *Cognitive Linguistics* 14 (4): 281–320.

Panther, Klaus-Uwe, and Günter Radden, eds. 1999. *Metonymy in Language and Thought*. Amsterdam: John Benjamins.

Pérez Hernández, Lorena. 2013. "Approaching the utopia of a global brand. The relevance of image schemas as multimodal resources for the branding industry". *Review of Cognitive Linguistics* 11 (2): 285–302.

Pérez Hernández, Lorena. 2014. "Cognitive grounding for cross-cultural commercial communication". *Cognitive Linguistics* 25 (2): 203–248.

Peréz-Rull, Carmelo. 2001. "The emotional control metaphors". *Journal of English Studies* 3 (2): 179–192.

References

Pérez-Sobrino, Paula 2017. *Multimodal Metaphor and Metonymy in Advertising*. Amsterdam: John Benjamins.

Pinar Sanz, María Jesús, ed. 2013. *Multimodality and Cognitive Linguistics*. Special Issue of *Review of Cognitive Linguistics* 11 (2). Amsterdam: John Benjamins.

Pollaroli, Chiara, and Andrea Rocci. 2015. "The argumentative relevance of pictorial and multimodal metaphor in advertising". *Journal of Argumentation in Context* 4 (2):158–199.

Popova, Yanna. 2005. "Image schemas and verbal synaesthesia". In *From Perception to Meaning*, edited by Beate Hampe, 2005b, 395–419. Berlin: Mouton de Gruyter.

Potsch, Elisabeth, and Robert F. Williams. 2012. "Image schemas and conceptual metaphor in action comics". In *Linguistics and the Study of Comics*, edited by Frank Bramlett, 3–36. London: Palgrave Macmillan.

Richardson, Daniel, and Teenie Matlock. 2007. "The integration of figurative language and static depictions: An eye movement study of fictive motion". *Cognition* 102 (1): 129–138.

Ritchie, David L. 2008. "x is a journey: Embodied simulation in metaphor interpretation". *Metaphor and Symbol* 23 (3): 174–199.

Robbins, Philip, and Murat Aydede, eds. 2009. *Cambridge Handbook of Situated Cognition*. New York: Cambridge University Press.

Sinha, Chris, and Kristine Jensen de López. 2000. "Language, culture and the embodiment of spatial cognition". *Cognitive Linguistics* 11 (1/2): 17–41.

Šorm, Ester, and Gerard Steen 2013. "Processing visual metaphor: A study in thinking out loud". *Metaphor and the Social World* 3 (1), 1–34.

Sweetser, Eve. 1990. *From Etymology to Pragmatics. Metaphorical and Cultural Aspects of Semantic Structure*. Cambridge: Cambridge University Press.

Szawerna, Michał. 2017. *Metaphoricity of Conventionalized Diegetic Images in Comics. A Study in Multimodal Cognitive Linguistics*. Frankfurt am Main: Peter Lang.

Talmy, Leonard. 1996. "Fictive motion in language and 'ception'". In *Language and Space. Language, Speech, and Communication*, edited by Paul Bloom, Mary Peterson, Lynn Nadel, and Merrill Garrett, 211–276. Cambridge, MA: MIT Press.

Talmy, Leonard. 1988. "Force dynamics in language and cognition". *Cognitive Science* 12 (1): 49–100.

Talmy, Leonard. 2003. "The representation of spatial structure in spoken and signed language: A neural model". *Language and Linguistics* 4 (2): 207–250.

Thornburg, Linda, and Klaus Panther. 1997. "Speech act metonymies". In *Discourse and Perspective in Cognitive Linguistics*, edited by Wolf-Andreas Liebert, Gisele Reddeker, and Linda Waugh, 205–219. Amsterdam: John Benjamins.

Tseng, Ming-Yu. 2017. "Primary metaphors and multimodal metaphors of food: Examples from an intercultural food design event". *Metaphor and Symbol* 32 (3): 211–229.

Tseronis, Assimakis, and Charles Forceville. 2017a. "Argumentation and rhetoric in visual and multimodal communication". In *Multimodal Argumentation and Rhetoric in Media Genres*, edited by Assimakis, Tseronis, and Charles Forceville, 2017b, 1–24. Amsterdam: John Benjamins.

Tseronis, Assimakis, and Charles Forceville, eds. 2017b. *Multimodal Argumentation and Rhetoric in Media Genres*. Amsterdam: John Benjamins.

References

Türker, Ebru. 2013. "A corpus-based approach to emotion metaphors in Korean: A case study of anger, happiness, and sadness". *Review of Cognitive Linguistics* 11(1): 73–144.

Winkielman, Piotr, Seana Coulson, and Paula Niedentha. 2018. "Dynamic grounding of emotion concepts". *Philosophical Transactions, Royal Society B* 373: 20170127. doi: 10.1098/rstb.2017.0127

Winter, Bodo. 2014. "Horror movies and the cognitive ecology of primary metaphors". *Metaphor and Symbol* 29 (3): 151–170.

Winter, Bodo, and Teenie Matlock. 2017. "Primary metaphors are both cultural and embodied". In *Metaphor, Embodied Cognition, and Discourse*, edited by Beate Hampe, 2017b, 99–115. Cambridge: Cambridge University Press.

Yu, Ning. 2009. "Nonverbal and multimodal manifestations of metaphors and metonymies: A case study". In *Multimodal Metaphor*, edited by Charles Forceville, and Eduardo Urios-Aparisi, 2009b, 119–143. Berlin: Mouton de Gruyter.

Yu, Ning. 2017. "LIFE AS OPERA: A cultural metaphor in Chinese". In *Advances in Cultural Linguistics* edited by Farzad Sharifian, 65–87. Singapore: Springer Nature. doi: 10.1007/978-981-10-4056-6_4.

Yu, Ning, and Jia, Dingding. 2016. "Metaphor in culture: LIFE IS A SHOW in Chinese". *Cognitive Linguistics* 27 (2): 146–179.

Zbikowski, Lawrence M. 2000 "*Des Herzraums Abschied*: Mark Johnson's theory of embodied knowledge and music theory". *Theory and Practice* 22 (23): 1–16.

Zbikowski, Lawrence M. 2009. "Music, language, and multimodal metaphor". In *Multimodal Metaphor*, edited by Charles Forceville, and Eduardo Urios-Aparisi, 2009b, 359–381. Berlin: Mouton de Gruyter.

Zlatev Jordan, Johan Blomberg, and Ulf Magnusson. 2012. "Metaphor and subjective experience. A study of motion-emotion metaphors in English, Swedish, Bulgarian, and Thai". In *Moving Ourselves, Moving others. Motion and Emotion in Intersubjectivity, Consciousness and Language*, edited by Ad Foolen, Ulrike M. Lüdke, Timothy P. Racine, and Jordan Zlatev, 423–450. Amsterdam: John Benjamins.

Dictionaries

Wielki Słownik Języka Polskiego (WSJP), the online version: www.wsjp.pl/

Data sources

Kapusta, Janusz. 2014. *Plus Minus. Podręcznik do myślenia* [*Plus Minus. A handbook for thinking*]. Poznań: Zysk i S-ka.

Plus Minus, March 5, 2011 (Example 3.10 'In the theatre of life everybody plays the main part').

Plus Minus, November 30, 2013 (Example 2.4 'Falling in love—conversely to gravitation. It attracts more, the more distant they are').

Plus Minus, January 17, 2015 (Example 3.3 'In the journey of life, all tickets are one-way').

Plus Minus, August 6, 2016 (Example 3.8 'Life is not an Olympic competition. It gives many more awards than three medals').

Plus Minus, August 12, 2017 (Example 3.12 'Life is like a canvas. One will paint a masterpiece on it, another—a shoddy/cheap picture').

Plus Minus, April 21, 2018 (Example 3.9 'Life is a game in which the winner always loses').

Index

Note: Page numbers in *italics* indicate figures and page numbers in **bold** indicate tables.

Abdel-Raheem, Ahmed 49, 79
abstract concepts: cognitive linguistics and 7; film and 63; genre in 74–75; metaphors and 22–23; metonymy and 22–23; multimodality in 8–9; spatialization of 8–9; visual thinking and xii
ABSTRACT IDEAS ARE OBJECTS metaphor 31, 60
ACTION IS MOTION metaphor 50, 71n5
ACTIONS, metonymic activation of 29
activation indicators 10, **11**, 22, 55
affordances of the pictorial mode 32, 37, 42, 45, 78
ARGUMENT 49
Arnheim, Rudolph xii
ATTRIBUTE FOR OBJECT/THING (HAVING THAT ATTRIBUTE) metonymy 63
ATTRIBUTE schema 19n22
AWARENESS concept 57–58

BAD IS DARK metaphor 20n25, 44, 63
BALANCE schema 2, 4, 39, 60
Barenboim, Daniel 66, 67
Barsalou, Lawrence W. 18n7
Bateman, John A. 12, 17, 18n15, 19n23, 47n19, 70n2, 79
BEHAVIOURAL SYMPTOM FOR CAUSE metonymy 40
BEHAVIOURAL SYMPTOM FOR EMOTION metonymy 40

BIG-SMALL schema 41, 56, 79
Blomberg, Johan 24
Body in the Mind, The (Johnson) 1
BODY IS THE CONTAINER FOR EMOTIONS metaphor 22, 28, 41–42
BOUNDED SPACE schema 31, 37–39, 58, 62, 66, 78; *see also* CONTAINER schema
BRIGHT-DARK schema 20n25; *see also* LIGHT-DARK schema

Calbris, Geneviève 8
CAREER IS A JOURNEY metaphor 49, 71n6
cartoons *13*, *16*, *26*, 27, *30*, 33–36, *38*, *39*, *40*, *43*, *49*, *51*, *53*, *54*, *56*, *57*, *59*, *61*, *62*, *65*, *66*; abstract concepts and 9; EMOTION concepts in 24, *26*, 26–28, 29–30, *30*, 31–34, *34*, 35, *35*, 36–38, *38*, *39*, 39–42, 42, *40*, *42*, 44, 45; image-schematic metaphors in 1, 8; LIFE concepts in 49–51, *51*, 52–53, *53*, *54*, 55–56, *56*, 57, *57*, 58, *59*, 59–61, *61*, 62, *62*, 64–65, *65*, *66*; static visuo-spatial modality of 24, 73–74; as verbo-pictorial aphorisms 1, 8, 10; *see also* verbo-pictorial aphorisms
CAUSED MOTION schema *see* MOTION schema
CAUSES ARE FORCES metaphor 31, 36, 60
CENTRE-PERIPHERY schema 4

Index 93

CHANGE OF STATE IS A CHANGE OF LOCATION metaphor 41, 60
"Chociaż mamy nieskończoną ilość dróg do wyboru i tak pójdziemy tylko jedną" 51
Cienki, Alan 5, 8, 13
co-expressiveness across modes 23; see also multimodal discourse
cognitive linguistics xii, 1, 6–8, 17, 22–23
Colston, Herbert L. 23
comics 24, 43, 49
communication xii, 49
COMPULSION schema 3, 3
conceptual metaphors see metaphors, conceptual
conceptual metaphor theory (CMT) 7, 23, 46n15, 64, 69, 71n14
conceptual metonymy see metonymy, conceptual
CONTAINER schema 15, 31, 40; see also BOUNDED SPACE schema
CONTAINMENT schema 5–6
conventional metaphor see metaphors, conventional
CORRECT IS STRAIGHT metaphor 13
creative reworking (of metaphor): EMOTION concepts and 22, 52; LIFE concepts and 58; multimodal 69; persuasion and 76; symbolic condensation and 78; verbo-pictorial aphorisms and 34, 44, 48, 57, 68, 77
cultural model of LIFE; see LIFE, cultural model
CYCLE schema 4, 37
"Człowiek jak butelka—ma znaczenie. Dopóki ma coś w sobie" 16

Dąbrowska, Dorota 79
Dancygier, Barbara 47n21
Damasio, Antonio 24
DARKNESS 63
DEPRESSION 63
DESIRE 35
DESPAIR 22, 42–44
DIFFICULTIES ARE BURDENS metaphor 40–41
DIFFICULTIES ARE IMPEDIMENTS TO MOTION metaphor 41
"Dostajemy ileś czasu na zaistnienie jak dźwięk" 66

Droga (The Road) 71n6
dynamic category of metaphors 10–11, 11, 32, 39; see also metaphoricity

EFFECT FOR CAUSE metonymy 40
EFFECT OF EMOTION FOR THE EMOTION (CAUSE) metonymy 28, 74
embodied artifacts 5–6
embodied cognition 18n7
EMOTIONAL DIFFICULTIES 41
EMOTIONAL DIFFICULTIES ARE BURDENS metaphor 42
EMOTIONAL DIFFICULTIES ARE IMPEDIMENTS TO MOTION metaphor 42
EMOTIONAL/INTERPERSONAL DISTANCE IS (PHYSICAL) DISTANCE metaphor 18n10, 22, 26–30
EMOTIONAL RELATIONSHIPS 25
EMOTIONAL STATES ARE OBJECTS/ LOCATIONS metaphor 22, 30–32, 42
EMOTION frame 41–42
EMOTION METAPHOR SYSTEM 26
EMOTIONS: abstract concepts and 44; as cognitive cultural models 23; cognitive linguistics and 23; defining 24–25; DESIRE 35; DESPAIR 22, 42–44; FALLING IN LOVE 32–33; HAPPINESS 22, 38–39, 44–45; HOPE 22, 42–44; image schemas and 22; LONELINESS 22, 30, 44; LOVE 22, 32–37, 44; multimodality in 23; NEAR-FAR schema 25–26; PAIN 22, 36–37, 44; REAL WORRIES 40–42; SADNESS 41; STATE vs. PROCESS 24–25; UNHAPPINESS 22, 38–39, 44–45; verbo-gestural co-expressiveness and 23, 45n1; verbo-pictorial expression of 22, 25–45; WORRIES 22, 41, 44
EMOTIONS ARE BONDS metaphor 28–29, 31–32
EMOTIONS ARE ENCLOSURES/ BOUNDED SPACES 31–32, 37
EMOTIONS ARE FORCES metaphor 22, 28–29, 32, 36–37, 42–43
EMOTION scenario 31, 41
Evans, Vyvyan 4

EVENTS, metonymic activation of 29
EVENTS AS ACTIONS metaphor 60
EVENT STRUCTURE METAPHOR SYSTEM 41
experiential cognition 18n7

FAILURE IN LIFE 58
FALLING DOWN, metonymic activation of 60
FALLING IN LOVE 32–33
FALLING IN LOVE IS A FORCE-DYNAMIC ENCOUNTER (OF TWO PERSONS) metaphor 33
FEELING concepts 22, 24–25, 37, 44
FEELING OF PAIN 36
FEELINGS (PHYSICAL SENSATIONS) ARE FORCES metaphor 36–37
fictive motion 70n3
figure-ground reversal 41, 53
film 7, 62–63, 68–69
"*Film zwany życiem potrzebuje i światła i ciemności*" 62
Foolen, Ad 22
FORCE schema 2–5, 13–15, 37, 39, 60
Forceville, Charles 8, 12, 24, 63, 68, 74, 76
FRONT-BACK schema 14
Fuchs, Thomas 10

GAME concept 60
genre: abstract concepts and 74; animation 71n6; film 63, 73; metonymy and 29, 66; multimodal 10; specificity of cartoon 27, 45, 64, 76; static composition and 8, 20n24, 29, 43, 45, 74; verbo-pictorial 1, 9, 24–25, 45, 51, 63, 70, 73–75, 80n1
gestures 23
Gibbs, Raymond W. 17, 23, 71n5
GOAL DIRECTED MOTION 14
GOOD IS LIGHT/BRIGHT metaphor 20n25, 44, 63
Górska, Elżbieta 8, 11
Grady, Joseph E. 18n9, 20n25
GRASP schema 39
GRAVITATIONAL FORCE 34
Green, Melanie 4
grounded cognition 18n7

Hampe, Beate 17
HAPPINESS 22, 38–39, 44–45, 79
HAPPINESS IS UP 38
HAPPINESS IS HOLDING A LINE STRETCHED ACROSS A PRECIPICE AND BALANCING ON A ROPE STRETCHED ABOVE IT (THE PRECIPICE) metaphor 38
HAPPY IS LIGHT/BRIGHT metaphor 20n25, 63
Hidalgo-Downing, Laura 76
HOPE 22, 42–44
HOPE AND DESPAIR ARE FORCES metaphor 44
HUMAN RELATIONSHIPS ARE FORCES metaphor 32

iconic coding 11, 19n19
iconicity 77–78
IDEAS ARE OBJECTS metaphor 12
IGNORANCE IS DARKNESS metaphor 63
image schemas: abstract concepts and 5; ATTRIBUTE 19n22; BALANCE 2, 4, 39, 60; BIG-SMALL 41, 56, 79; BOUNDED SPACE 31, 37–39, 58, 62, 65, 78; BRIGHT-DARK 20n25; CAUSED MOTION 37, CENTRE-PERIPHERY 4; clusters of 4, 31, 39, 58, 60, 65, 68; COMPULSION 3, *3*; concept of 1–5; CONTAINER 5–6, 15, 31; CYCLE 4, 37; defining 6; embodiment of 5–7; emotion concepts and 22; experiential 4, **4**; FORCE 2–5, 13–15, 37, 39, 60; FRONT-BACK 14; gestalt structures in 4; GRASP 39; ITERATION 4–5; LIGHT-DARK 15, 63–64; LINK 28, 31, 33, 35, 37, 78; LONG-SHORT 13; MOTION 15, 39, 48, 58, 60; multimodal analysis of 15; NEAR-FAR 2, 4, 25–28, 33–35, 37; OBJECT 13–15, 65; PART-WHOLE 37; PATH 3–4, 13–15, 39, 48–50, 52, 55–56, 58, 68; PROCESS 4; product design and 21n29; PROXIMITY 17n2; REMOVAL OF RESTRAINT 3, *3*; SCALE 4, 15, 56–57; SELF-PROPELLED MOTION 68; sensory systems and

8; socio-cultural situatedness of 5–7; spatialization of 17n3; STRAIGHT 13, 39; SUPPORT 39, 60; TOWARD-AWAY FROM 2; UP-DOWN 16, 20n28–21n28, 38–39, 56, 60, 62, 78–79; VERTICALITY 20n28 image-schematic metaphors: cultural representation in 6–7; embodiment of 17; multimodality in 8, 16; reworking of 22, 48, 68
IMPORTANT IS BIG metaphor 53
IMPORTANT/SIGNIFICANT IS UP metaphor 62
INSTRUMENT FOR ACTION metonymy 28, 33, 45, 74
INTENSITY OF AN EMOTIONAL STATE IS THE SIZE OF THE CONTAINER metaphor 41
INTIMACY IS CLOSENESS metaphor 18n10
ITERATION schema 4–5

Jensen de López, Kristine 5–6
Jeulink, Marloes 8, 68
Johnson, Christopher 18n9
Johnson, Mark: on creative metaphors 64; emotion concepts and 22–23; image schemas 1–6, 16–17, 17n2, 17n3, 19n22; LIFE concepts 68; on music 8; on orientational metaphors 18n4; on primary metaphors 18n9, 50
JOURNEY, metonymic activation of 39–40, 55; verbo-pictorial activation 58

Kapusta, Janusz: abstract concepts and xii, 1, 74; emotion concepts and 22, 44–45; iconic coding and 78; multimodal discourse of 77; *Plus Minus. Podręcznik do Myślenia* 9–10, *10*, 75; symbolic condensation of 78; temporal concepts of 74; verbo-pictorial aphorisms of 9–10, 12–13, *13*, 14, *16*, 15–17, 24, *27*, *30*, *33*, *34*, *35*, *36*, *38*, *39*, *40*, 44–45, 48–49, *49*, *51*, *53*, *54*, *56*, *57*, 58, *59*, *61*, *62*, 64–65, *65*, 68; visual thinking of xii, xiii
K-dron xiii
Kijowicz, Mirosław 71n6

Kimmel, Michael 6
Kjeldsen, Jens E. 78
Klee, Paul 8
KNOWING IS SEEING metaphor 44, 57, 63
KNOWLEDGE IS LIGHT metaphor 63
Koch, Sabine C. 10
Kolter, Astrid 10
Kövecses, Zoltán xii, 7, 17, 18n10, 19n24, 23, 26–28, 31, 32, 34
Kraljevic-Mujic, Blanca 76
Kuczok, Marcin 69

Ladewig, Silva H. 10
Lakoff, George xii, 5–8, 15, 17n1, 18n4, 18n9, 20n24, 22–23, 30, 31, 34, 41, 43, 46n7, 47n21, 48–50, 52, 55, 61, 64, 67–69, 71n5, 71n10
Langacker, Ronald W. xii, 7, 19n24, 46n10, 70n3
language: emotion concepts and 22–23; iconicity in 77–78; image schemas and 5–6; signed 77–78; spatial foundations of 7
Larson, Steve 8
LIFE, cultural model of 41, 50, 52, 55, 72n16, 72n22
LIFE GOALS ARE DESTINATIONS metaphor 49
LIFE IS A (THEATRE) PLAY metaphor 61–62, 67
LIFE IS A BURDEN metaphor 67
LIFE IS A COMPROMISE metaphor 69
LIFE IS A DAY metaphor 67
LIFE IS A GAME metaphor 48, 58, 60–61, 67, 69
LIFE IS A JOURNEY metaphor 49–50, 51–53, 55, 57–58, 67–69, 71n5
LIFE IS A MOVIE metaphor 62, 72n16
LIFE IS AN OPERA metaphor 72n22
LIFE IS A PIECE OF ART metaphor 65
LIFE IS A PRECIOUS POSSESSION metaphor 67, 69
LIFE IS A SHOW/ENTERTAINMENT metaphor 48, 58, 61–62, 69
LIFE IS A STORY metaphor 67
LIFE IS A STRUGGLE metaphor 69
LIFE IS A YEAR metaphor 67
LIFE IS BONDAGE metaphor 67
LIFE IS COMPROMISE metaphor 67

LIFE IS FLUID IN THE BODY metaphor 67
LIFE IS LIGHT metaphor 57–58, 67
LIFE IS WAR metaphor 67
LIFE JOURNEY IS A ONE WAY TRIP IN A PUBLIC TRANSPORT VEHICLE metaphor 53
LIGHT 63
LIGHT-DARK schema 15, 63–64; *see also* BRIGHT-DARK schema
LINK schema 28, 31, 33, 35, 37, 78
Littlemore, Jeanette xii, 20n20
LIVING A LIFE IS A CREATIVE PROCESS metaphor 65
LOCATION EVENT-STRUCTURE metaphor 52, 71n5
LONELINESS 22, 30, 44
LONG-SHORT schema 13
LONG-TERM PURPOSEFUL ACTIVITY 71n5
LOSING SUCCESS IS FALLING DOWN metaphor 60
LOVE 22, 32–37, 44, 49
LOVE IS A JOURNEY metaphor 49, 71n6
LOVE IS AN ENCLOSURE OF TWO PEOPLE WITHIN A RECTANGLE metaphor 36–37
LOVE IS BOND metaphor 33, 35, 37
LOVE IS CLOSENESS metaphor 33–35, 37
LOVE IS FIRE metaphor 34–35
LOVE IS FORCE metaphor 34
LOVE IS UNITY metaphor 37

Magnusson, Ulf 24
MAKING CHOICES (IN LIFE) IS MAKING DECISION ABOUT WHICH WAY TO GO metaphor 51
MAKING ERRORS 14
Matlock, Teenie 6–7, 18n9
MEANS ARE PATHS metaphor 52
metaphorical entailments 46n15, 64–65
metaphoricity: activation indicators 10–11, **11**, 22, 55; activation of 9–10, 17; defined 10; dynamic 9–10, 16–17, 22, 33, 48, 70; gradable 11, 48, 70; verbo-pictorial aphorisms and 75
metaphors: abstract concepts and 22; conceptual theory of 23; cultural representation in 6–7; dynamic approach to 10–11, **11**, 17, 19n16, 45, 48, 70, 76; EMOTION concepts and 23; folk model of 50–51; gestures and 23; image-schematic 6–8, 22, 48; LIFE concepts and 68–69; modality-independent nature of 24; monomodal 11, **11**, 32–34, 45, 68, 70, 75; multimodal 11, **11**, 13–14, 17, 75, 77; non-verbal 11; orientational 18n4; as persuasion 76; primary 6–8, 18n9, 20n25, 50, 60, 63, 73, 78–79; reworking of 22, 34, 44, 48, 52, 57–58, 68–69, 76–78; semiotic modes of xii; sleeping 10–11, 26, 29; verbal 9, 11, 19n18, 23, 34, 69, 72n14; verbo-musical 67; verbo-pictorial 36, 73, 77; waking 10–11, 27, 29, 51, 53; *see also* conceptual metaphor theory (CMT)
metaphors, conceptual: ABSTRACT IDEAS AS OBJECTS 31, 60; ACTION IS MOTION 50, 71n5; BAD IS DARK (DARKNESS) 20n25, 44, 63; NEGATIVE IS BLACK (DARK)14; BODY IS THE CONTAINER FOR EMOTIONS 22, 28, 41–42; CAREER IS A JOURNEY 71n6; CAUSES ARE FORCES 31, 36, 60; CHANGE OF STATE IS A CHANGE OF LOCATION 41, 60; CORRECT IS STRAIGHT 13; DESIRE IS PHYSIOLOGICAL FORCE 35; DIFFICULTIES ARE BURDENS 40–41; DIFFICULTIES ARE IMPEDIMENTS TO MOTION 41; EMOTION concepts and 22; EMOTIONAL DIFFICULTIES ARE BURDENS 42; EMOTIONAL DIFFICULTIES ARE IMPEDIMENTS TO MOTION 42; EMOTIONAL/ INTERPERSONAL DISTANCE IS (PHYSICAL) DISTANCE 18n10, 22, 26–29; EMOTIONAL STATES ARE OBJECTS/LOCATIONS 22, 30–32, 42; EMOTIONS ARE BONDS 28–29, 31–32; EMOTIONS ARE FORCES 22,

28–29, 31, 32, 36–37, 42–43; EMOTIONS ARE ENCLOSURES 31–32; EVENTS AS ACTIONS 60; EVENT STRUCTURE SYSTEM 41; FEELING concepts and 22; FEELINGS (PHYSICAL SENSATIONS) ARE FORCES 36–37; GOOD IS LIGHT/BRIGHT 20n25, 44, 63; HAPPY IS LIGHT/BRIGHT 20n25, 63; HOPE AND DESPAIR ARE FORCES 44; HUMAN RELATIONSHIPS ARE FORCES 32; IDEAS ARE OBJECTS 12; IGNORANCE IS DARKNESS 63; IMPORTANT IS BIG 53; IMPORTANT/SIGNIFICANT IS UP 62; INTIMACY IS CLOSENESS 18n10; KNOWING IS SEEING 44, 57, 63; KNOWLEDGE IS LIGHT 63; LIFE GOALS ARE DESTINATIONS 49, 51; LIFE IS A (THEATRE) PLAY 61–62, 67; LIFE IS A BURDEN 67; LIFE IS A COMPROMISE 69; LIFE IS A DAY 67; LIFE IS A GAME 48, 58, 60–61, 67, 69; LIFE IS A JOURNEY 49–50, 52–53, 55, 57–58, 67–69, 71n5; LIFE IS A MOVIE 62, 72n16; LIFE IS AN OPERA 72n22; LIFE IS A PIECE OF ART 65; LIFE IS A PRECIOUS POSSESSION 67, 69; LIFE IS A SHOW/ENTERTAINMENT 48, 58, 61–62, 69; LIFE IS A STORY 67; LIFE IS A STRUGGLE 69; LIFE IS A YEAR 67; LIFE IS BONDAGE 67; LIFE IS COMPROMISE 67; LIFE IS FLUID IN THE BODY 67; LIFE IS LIGHT 57–58, 67; LIFE IS WAR 67; LIFE IS A JOURNEY 49–50, 51–53, 55, 57–58, 67–69, 71n5; LOCATION EVENT-STRUCTURE 52, 71n5; LOSING SUCCESS IS FALLING DOWN 60–61; LOVE IS A JOURNEY 71n6; LOVE IS BOND 33, 35, 37; LOVE IS CLOSENESS 33–35, 37; LOVE IS FIRE 34–35; LOVE IS FORCE 34; LOVE IS UNITY 37; MAKING CHOICES (IN LIFE) IS MAKING DECISION ABOUT WHICH WAY TO GO 51–52; MAKING ERRORS IS MOTION ALONG A NON-STRAIGHT PATH 14; MEANS ARE PATHS 52; MOVING EGO MODEL OF TIME 56–57; MOVING TIME 15; NEGATIVE IS DOWN 38, 79; POSITIVE IS UP 16, 38, 79; POSITIVE IS WHITE (BRIGHT/LIGHT) 14; PROGRESS IS MOTION FORWARD 55; PURPOSEFUL ACTIVITIES IS A JOURNEY 51; PURPOSES ARE DESTINATIONS 50, 71n5; SAD IS DARK 20n25, 63; SAD IS DOWN 41, 42; SADNESS IS A BURDEN 41, 42; SIMILARITY IS CLOSENESS 52; SOCIAL DISTANCE IS PHYSICAL DISTANCE 6–7; STATES ARE LOCATIONS/CONTAINERS/BOUNDED SPACES 31, 36, 38–39, 55, 62; SUCCESS IS UP 60; SUCCESS/FAILURE IN LIFE IS WINNING/LOSING IN A GAME 58; VISUAL FIELDS ARE CONTAINERS 43; WRONG IS NOT STRAIGHT 13

metaphors, conventional: combination of 44, 68; creative reworking of 22, 34, 44, 48, 52, 58, 68, 76–78; elaboration of 42, 44, 62, 69, 77; extension of 44, 53, 69, 77; human experience and 26; metaphoricity of 11; multimodal metaphors and 13–14, 28; questioning 58, 60; *see also* metaphors, conceptual

metaphors, creative: FALLING IN LOVE AS A FORCE-DYNAMIC ENCOUNTER (OF TWO PERSONS) 33, HAPPINESS IS HOLDING A LINE STRETCHED ACROSS A PRECIPICE AND BALANCING ON A ROPE STRETCHED ABOVE IT (THE PRECIPICE) 38; INTENSITY OF AN EMOTIONAL STATE IS THE SIZE OF THE CONTAINER 41; LIFE JOURNEY IS A ONE WAY TRIP IN A PUBLIC TRANSPORT VEHICLE 53; LIVING A LIFE IS A CREATIVE PROCESS 65; LOVE IS AN ENCLOSURE OF TWO

PEOPLE WITHIN A RECTANGLE 36–37; NIGHTMARES (OF THE PAST) ARE FORCES MOVING TOWARDS THE EGO FROM BEHIND 15; NOT BEING MISTAKEN IN LIFE IS SELF-PROPELLED MOTION FORWARD ALONG A SINGLE STRAIGHT PATH 13; PAIN IS AN ENCLOSURE OF AN INDIVIDUAL WITHIN A CIRCLE 36–37; PASSING IN LIFE IS MOTION FORWARD ALONG A HORIZONTAL PATH COINCIDING WITH THE MOTION DOWNWARD ALONG THE VERTICAL PATH OF AN EGO DISAPPEARING IN THE GROUND 56–57; PERSON LIVING A LIFE IS A PAINTER, THE 65; PURPOSEFUL ACTIVITY OF THE WORLD 50–51; SIGNIFICANCE OF A HUMAN BEING IS THE CONTENT OF THE CONTAINER 16; TIMESPAN OF A HUMAN LIFE IS THE DURATION OF A SOUND, THE 66; TRAVELLER IS THE (CHANGING) LANDSCAPE, THE 53; UNFULFILLED DREAMS ARE FORCES MOVING TOWARDS THE EGO FROM THE FRONT 15
metaphors, multimodal *see* multimodal metaphor
metonymic vehicle: double pictorial 33, 40, 55; mental contact and 20n24; multiple 57; pictorial mode 15–16, 29, 44, 66, 68, 74
metonymy: abstract concepts and 22; activation of metaphoric source domains 13, 15, 20n24, 29, 31, 33, 39–40, 43, 50, 52, 55, 58, 61, 63, 65, 68, 73–74; conceptual theory of 13, 19n24, 23; EMOTION concepts and 23, 28, 29; modality-independent nature of 24; semiotic modes of xii; theory of 19n24–20n24; verbal mode and 9; verbo-pictorial discourse and 73–74
metonymy, conceptual: ACTION FOR OBJECT INVOLVED IN THE ACTION 23; ATTRIBUTE FOR OBJECT/THING (HAVING THAT ATTRIBUTE) 63; BEHAVIOURAL SYMPTOM FOR CAUSE 40; BEHAVIOURAL SYMPTOM FOR EMOTION 40; CAUSE OF EMOTION FOR EMOTION 46n3; DOWNWARD BODILY ORIENTATION FOR SADNESS 46n14; EFFECT FOR CAUSE 40; EFFECT OF EMOTION FOR THE EMOTION (CAUSE) 28, 74; INSTRUMENT FOR ACTION 28, 33, 45, 74; INSTRUMENT FOR SOUND 66; LOCATION FOR OBJECT 23; OBJECT INVOLVED IN THE ACTION FOR THE ACTION 74; PART FOR WHOLE 20n24; PATH FOR MOTION 13–14, 20n26, 39, 74; RESULT FOR ACTION 44; (REPRESENTATIVE) STAGE OF AN ACTION FOR THE ACTION 29, 31, 45, 61, 74; SUBEVENT FOR THE EVENT 45
"*Miłość jest ogniem, który gasi pragnienie*" 35
"*Miłość to grawitacja wszechświatów o twarzach ludzi*" 34
Mittelberg, Irene 8, 9 20n.24, 23, 73
modes/modality 18n12
monomodal metaphor 11, **11**, 32–34, 45, 68, 70, 75
MOTION ALONG A NON-STRAIGHT PATH 14
MOTION schema 14–15, 39, 48, 58, 60, 70n3
MOVIE 63–64
MOVING EGO MODEL OF TIME 56–57
MOVING TIME 15
"*Można zrobić wiele błędów, ale nie warto się pomylić*" 13
Müller, Cornelia 7, 9–11, 19n17, 19n18, 22–23, 26–27, 45n1, 46n17, 76
multimodal discourse: abstract concepts in 8, 74; EMOTION concepts in 22; genre in 74–76; image-schematic analysis of 79; metaphoricity in 22; pictorial-mode-first procedure

75; symbolic condensation and 78;
verbal-mode-first procedure 75;
verbo-pictorial aphorisms in 1, 74–78
multimodal metaphor: complementarity
  in 17; conventional metaphor in 13;
  co-verbal 78; metaphoricity of 11, **11**;
  monomodal metaphor and 11, 75, 78;
  overlap in 17; PATH schema in 49;
  text-image relations and 14; verbo-
  musical 67; verbo-pictorial 36, 73, 77
MUSIC 67
MUSICAL SOUND 67

"*Nadzieja poszerza, rozpacz zawęża*" 44
NEAR-FAR schema 2, 4, 25–28,
  33–35, 37
NEGATIVE IS DOWN metaphor 38, 79
NEGATIVE IS BLACK (DARK)
  metaphor 14
"*Nic nie łączy bardziej ludzi niż uczucie
  i nic też ich bardziej nie rozdziela*" 27
non-verbal metaphors 11
NOT BEING MISTAKEN IN LIFE
  IS SELF-PROPELLED MOTION
  FORWARD ALONG A SINGLE
  STRAIGHT PATH 13

OBJECT INVOLVED IN THE
  ACTION FOR THE ACTION
  metonymy 74
OBJECT schema 13–14, 65
orientational metaphors 18n4
Ortiz, María J. 8, 18n9, 63
Özaçalişkan, Şeyda 69

PAIN 22, 36–37, 44
PAIN IS AN ENCLOSURE OF AN
  INDIVIDUAL WITHIN A CIRCLE
  metaphor 36–37
PAINTING 64–65, 77
PAINTING CANVAS 65
Paling, Sissy 63
Panther, Klaus 20n24, 46n6
PART-WHOLE schema 37
PASSING IN LIFE metaphor 56–57
PATH FOR MOTION metonymy
  13–14, 20n26, 39, 74
PATH schema 3–4, 13–15, 39, 48–50,
  52, 55–56, 58, 68, 70n3

Pérez Hernández, Lorena 8
Pérez-Sobrino, Paula 12, 79
PERSON LIVING A LIFE IS
  A PAINTER, THE metaphor 65
PHYSIOLOGICAL FORCE OF
  THIRST 35
pictorial mode 18n12, 22, 32, 37, 41,
  45, 78
pictorial runes 24, 74
Plus Minus (journal) 9, 74
Plus Minus. Podręcznik do Myślenia
  (Kapusta) 9, *10*, 75
POSITIVE IS UP metaphor 16, 38, 79
POSITIVE IS WHITE (BRIGHT/
  LIGHT) 14
"*Prawdziwe zmartwienia podróżują
  razem z nami*" 39, 40
primary metaphors 6–8, 18n9, 20n25,
  50, 60, 63, 73, 78–79
PROCESS schema 4
PROTAGONIST'S LIFE GOALS
  metaphor 51
PROXIMITY schema 17n2
"*Przemijamy przez całe życie, ale pod
  koniec jakby bardziej*" 56
PURPOSES ARE DESTINATIONS
  metaphor 50–51, 71n5

Radden, Günter xii, 19n24, 46n6
REAL WORRIES 40–42, 79
REMOVAL OF RESTRAINT schema
  3, *3*
RESULT FOR ACTION metonymy 44
rhetoric: attention-grabbing effects in
  76; humorous/ironic effects in 32, 55;
  multimodal 45, 76; persuasion in 76;
  symbolic condensation and 78; verbal
  aphorisms and 35; verbo-musical
  metaphors and 67; visual 8, 73

SAD IS DARK metaphor 20n25, 63
SAD IS DOWN metaphor 41, 42
SADNESS IS A BURDEN metaphor
  41, 42
"*Samotność to stabilny stan człowieka,
  często nienaturalnie zachwiany,
  przyjaźniami, spotkaniami lub
  małżeństwem*" 30
SCALE schema 4, 15, 56–57

SELF-PROPELLED MOTION
  schema 68
signed language 77–78
SIGNIFICANT/IMPORTANT IS
  BIG 79
SIGNIFICANCE OF A HUMAN
  BEING metaphor 15
SIMILARITY IS CLOSENESS
  metaphor 52
simile 15, 66
Sinha, Chris 5–6
situated cognition 18n7
sleeping metaphors 10–11, 26, 29–30
SOCIAL DISTANCE IS PHYSICAL
  DISTANCE metaphor 6–7
SOUND 66, 74, 77
SOURCE-PATH-GOAL schema *see*
  PATH schema
STAGE OF ACTION FOR ACTION
  metonymy 29, 31, 45, 61, 74
STATES ARE LOCATIONS/
  CONTAINERS/BOUNDED SPACES
  metaphor 31, 36, 38–39, 55, 60–61
STRAIGHT schema 13, 39
SUBEVENT FOR THE EVENT
  metonymy 45
SUCCESS/FAILURE IN LIFE IS
  WINNING/LOSING IN A GAME
  metaphor 58
SUCCESS IS UP metaphor 60
Summa, Michela 10
SUPPORT schema 39, 60
Sweetser, Eve 43, 47n21, 63
"*Świat dokądś zmierza, co wcale nie
  oznacza, że idziemy w tym samym
  kierunku*" 49
symbolic condensation 78
Szawerna, Michał 43, 47n18, 71n12
"*Szczęście to linia rozpięta nad
  przepaścią, nieszczęście to przepaść
  rozpostarta pod liną*" 38

Tag, Susanne 10
Talmy, Leonard 77
text-image relations 12–17
TIME, metonymic activation of 29; *see
  also* MOVING EGO MODEL OF
  TIME, MOVING TIME
TIMESPAN OF A HUMAN LIFE IS
  THE DURATION OF A SOUND,
  THE metaphor 66

TOWARD-AWAY FROM schema 2;
  see also NEAR-FAR schema
TRAVELLER IS THE (CHANGING)
  LANDSCAPE, THE metaphor 53
Tseronis, Assimakis 74, 76
Turner, Mark 31, 46n7, 47n21, 48, 61,
  67–69, 71n10

UNHAPPINESS 22, 38–39, 44–45, 79
UNHAPPINESS IS DOWN 38
UP-DOWN schema 16, 20n28–21n28,
  38–39, 56, 60, 62, 78–79
Urios-Aparisi, Eduardo 8

verbal metaphors 9, 11, 19n17, 19n18,
  23, 34, 69, 72n14
verbal mode 9, 15–16, 18n12, 73
verbo-gestural co-expressiveness 23
verbo-musical metaphors 67
verbo-pictorial aphorisms: cartoons as
  1, 8–9; EMOTION concepts 25–45;
  iconicity in 77; image schemas
  and 14–17; LIFE concepts 49–53,
  55–58, 60–62; metaphoricity of 75;
  metonymy and 73–74; multimodal
  analysis of 9–10, 12–17, 74–78;
  primary metaphors in 73; *see also*
  cartoons
verbo-pictorial genres 24
verbo-pictorial metaphors 36, 73, 77;
  see also multimodal metaphor
VERTICALITY schema 20n28; *see also*
  UP-DOWN schema
VISUAL FIELDS ARE CONTAINERS
  metaphor 43
visual thinking xii, xiii

waking metaphors 10–11, 27, 29, 51, 53
POSITIVE IS WHITE (BRIGHT/
  LIGHT) metaphor 14
Winter, Bodo 6–7, 18n9
"*W miłości świat się zawęża do drugiej
  osoby, w bólu do siebie*" 36
WORRIES 22, 41, 44
"*W podróży przez życie to my
  sami jesteśmy zmieniającym się
  krajobrazem*" 54
"*W podróży życia wszystkie bilety są w
  jedną stronę*" 53
WRONG IS NOT STRAIGHT
  metaphor 13

"W teatrze życia wszyscy grają główną
    rolę" 61
"W życiu punkty przestankowe mogą
    być dłuższe niż podróż" 54
Yu, Ning 49, 72n22
"Zakochanie—odwrotnie niż grawitacja.
    Przyciąga im bardziej oddalonych
    tym silniej" 33
"Zbliżenie ma swój limit. Oddalenie nie
    zna granic" 26

Zlatev, Jordan 24
"Życie jak fontanna—wynurza się
    z ciemności i do niej powraca,
    świadome światła" 57
"Życie jest grą, w której zwycięzca
    zawsze przegrywa" 59
"Życie jest jak płótno malarskie. Jeden
    namaluje na nim arcydzieło, drugi
    tandetny obraz" 65
"Życie nie jest olimpiadą. Przyznaje
    o wiele więcej nagród niż trzy
    medale" 59

For Product Safety Concerns and Information please contact our EU
representative GPSR@taylorandfrancis.com
Taylor & Francis Verlag GmbH, Kaufingerstraße 24, 80331 München, Germany

www.ingramcontent.com/pod-product-compliance
Lightning Source LLC
Chambersburg PA
CBHW070740230426
43669CB00014B/2521